HULL
at
WAR

HULL *at* WAR

The Breedon Books
Publishing Company
Derby

First published in Great Britain by
The Breedon Books Publishing Company Limited
44 Friar Gate, Derby, DE1 1DA
1993

ISBN 1 873626 53 3

Printed and bound by the Bath Press Limited of Bath and London.
Covers printed by BDC Printing Services Limited of Derby.

Contents

Members of the 9th Battalion, Hampshire Regiment help to clear away bomb damage. *Imperial War Museum.*

Introduction

THIS book is an attempt to portray in photographs what it was like to live and work in Hull during World War Two and how this conflict directly affected the lives of every man, woman and child. It is not meant to be a definitive work in any way, as space does not permit it to be, but an attempt has been made to try to capture the atmosphere of those years, when this country fought for its very survival, and for a time, alone.

As well as concentrating on everyday life — forced to adapt to stringent demands of war with the enforced rationing of food, fuel and clothing, of Air Raid Precautions and duty with the Home Guard — this book has also tried to show something of the experiences of the men and women of Hull serving with the armed forces.

Whilst it would be impossible to portray every unit in which Hull people served, there are included in this book photographs of the East Riding Yeomanry, East Yorkshire Regiment, the ATS and, of course, vessels of the fishing fleet requisitioned for war service.

Photographs and information have been drawn from a wide range of sources and I should like to thank Jill Crowther of the Local Studies Department, Central Library; Mr J.G.Roberts, the Director of Leisure Services; and Mr Arthur Credland of the Maritime Heritage Centre. Sources for photographs include the Harry Cartlidge Collection, the ARP archive at the Central Library, Councillor Sydney Smith's albums and the Imperial War Museum. Where no source is credited it was not possible to trace.

So, welcome to a world frozen in time, the world of ITMA, the black-out and gravy-browned legs. As you stroll through these pages, take a magnifying glass with you. After all, you might see yourself, or someone you know, looking back at you. And if you are old enough to remember the events, why not share your experiences with those who weren't?

Clive Hardy
February 1992

Party-goers pose for the camera at Bricknell Avenue Civil Defence Depot, 18 December 1943. *Central Library Collection.*

The Road to War

IT is almost fifty years since the surrender of the Japanese, on 14 August 1945, finally brought to an end World War Two. But how did it begin? What were the chain of events that would lead to conflict on a global scale in which nearly 50 million people would die and man's inhumanity to man would plumb new depths of savagery?

The Treaty of Versailles had placed the responsibility for the outbreak of World War One firmly upon Germany and her allies. Under the terms of the Treaty, Germany was to be virtually disarmed, stripped of territory including her overseas empire and made to pay reparations assessed at 136,000 million gold marks (about £6,600 million in 1919).

The victorious countries, especially the French, were in no mood to be magnanimous in victory. The provinces of Alsace-Lorraine were ceded to France, Eupen and Malmedy went to Belgium, and Poland was given West Prussia and Posen. The Saar was placed under Allied military occupation along with the cities of Danzig and Memel, whilst North Schleswig was handed over to Denmark. A demilitarized zone was also established to include the Rhineland and part of the Ruhr.

In part payment of reparations, German industry was systematically robbed of machinery and equipment, her merchant marine relieved of some, if not all, of its finest ships and her railways forced to hand over locomotives and rolling stock.

Of the Treaty, Marshal Foch said, "This is not peace, it is an armistice for twenty years." He was to be proved right.

Of Germany's former allies, the once mighty Austria-Hungarian Empire came off worse. The empire had collapsed into anarchy before the end of the war, the central Hapsburg Government, which had for so long held together Serbs, Magyars, Austrians, Slovaks and a score of ethnic minorities, ceased to function.

The result was that the empire split into a number of successor states who then began to squabble among themselves over the position of new frontiers. Things were so bad that many people had no idea to which 'new' country they belonged and numerous units of the former Imperial Army simply disbanded as there was nowhere to go to officially demobilise.

Of Germany's other allies, the Ottoman Empire lost Armenia, which became an independent republic, Syria and the Lebanon which were placed under French mandate, and Palestine, Iraq and Transjordan to British mandate, whilst Saudi Arabia, Kuwait and the other Gulf states became independent kingdoms.

Bulgaria, the smallest of Germany's allies, was made to hand over territory to the newly-created country of Yugoslavia and to give Thrace to Greece.

In Eastern Europe, Finland, Estonia, Latvia, Lithuania were new states created following the collapse of Tsarist Russia and for a few years there also existed the Ukrainian Republic (1917-19) and the Federal Republic of Transcaucasia, comprising Georgia, Azerbaijan and Turkarmenia.

It had been hoped that in future, countries would be able to settle their differences through the League of Nations instead of on the battlefield. The League, with its headquarters in Geneva, had been set up specifically to promote international peace through collective security. Unhappily it failed, doomed almost from the start as the United States declined membership and took off down the road of isolationism, whilst Germany was not allowed to join and Japan would eventually leave.

The League's first real test came in September 1931, when Japan invaded China's northern province of Manchuria. The League dithered, debated and did nothing else, collective security was non-existent.

Three years later, in December 1934, fascist Italy used a minor frontier dispute on the border of Abyssinia and Italian Somaliland as a pretext to pour in troops, tanks and artillery into its colony. For ten months the Abyssinians appealed to the League to arbitrate. On 3 October 1935, the Italians invaded. The following month the League half-heartedly imposed economic and financial sanctions on Italy. It was too little too late.

At the end of April 1936, Emperor Haile Selassie made a final plea to the League for help. "I must still hold on until my tardy allies appear, and if they never come, then I say prophetically and without bitterness, the West will perish."

But Selassie's allies had no intention of coming to his country's aid as they had already sold Abyssinia down the river. In December 1935, Sir Samuel Hoare and his French opposite number, Pierre Laval, had concocted a scheme whereby Abyssinia would hand over two-thirds of her territory to Italy in the name of appeasement.

The Times, usually a supporter of appeasement denounced the proposals and Prime Minister Stanley Baldwin, albeit temporarily, sacked Hoare to save his own political neck. In May 1936, Italian troops entered the Abyssinian capital of Addis Ababa and the emperor fled into exile. Italy formally announced the annexation of Abyssinia, the first conquest in Benito Mussolini's dream of a new Roman Empire.

The Depression

IN October 1929, a brand new luxury apartment on New York's plush Fifth Avenue cost around £1,500 a week to rent and a ticket to one of the hit Broadway shows averaged out at 28 dollars. By the end of the following month, the Fifth Avenue rental had been slashed by 90 per cent and the theatre tickets were down in price to two to three dollars each. The financial crisis at the New York Stock Exchange had begun to bite.

American industry had grown rapidly, too rapidly in fact, since the end of World War One due to a deliberate policy of readily available loans from the Federal Reserve Bank. In Europe, United States loans between 1925 and 1929 amounted to a staggering 2,900 million dollars and although some countries, such as Great Britain, were feeling the effects from overseas competition for their traditional industries, others such as Czechoslovakia, Austria and Germany, were enjoying a period of relative prosperity.

In July 1929 the United States economy finally overheated. Supply outstripped demand, necessitating a reduction in output and redundancies which, in turn, led to investors losing confidence and sent share prices plummeting. By the end of October, 18,000 million dollars had been wiped off the share value of US companies, but this was only the beginning. Despite a price rally during early months of 1930, confidence again slipped and by June the market had entered a downward slide which would last unabated for 25 months and see the value of all stocks listed on Wall Street shrink from 90,000 million dollars to just under 16,000 million dollars. The effect of the Wall Street Crash would be felt worldwide.

In 1931, Europe was rocked by a banking crisis with the collapse of the Vienna Bank of Austria and a run on the German Reichsbank. In Britain, severe financial strain was placed on London and the Labour Government, already battling against a slump and a dole queue of 2 million, proved incapable of being able to put together a programme of economic measures. The Government resigned and Ramsay MacDonald, with a handful of Labour MPs, joined forces with the Conservatives to form a National Government.

One of Labour's more able members, Sir Oswald Mosley, Chancellor of the Duchy of Lancaster, had already left the Government because the Cabinet had failed to support his scheme to bring unemployment down with a programme of public works, a higher school leaving age, early retirement and the control of credit through the banks. Mosley and his followers formed the New Party which eventually became the British Union of Fascists.

At the height of the Depression there were nearly three million insured workers in the United Kingdom without jobs and thousands more who either did not, or were not, eligible for registration. In the South-East, one worker in nine was on the dole whilst in Lancashire, South Wales, Tyneside and Clydeside — where a reliance of work rested on traditional industries — unemployment was at one in three or four of the workforce. In Bishop Auckland, where once 28,000 miners had been employed in 35 pits, there were now only 13 pits still in production employing 6,500 men on a part-time basis.

Between 1931 and 1935 an unemployed man with a wife and three children to support could expect to receive 29s 3d a week benefit or 'transitional payments' once benefit had been exhausted. Transitional payments were subject to means testing, a particularly vicious piece of legislation in which the earnings, savings, pensions and other assets of a family were taken into account before an award was made.

It was automatically assumed that the assets of a family were available to support its unemployed members. Children, if in work, and if they lived at home, were expected to support out-of-work parents.

Recruiting for Hull's Civil Defence gets underway in 1938. The city was blessed with one of the few councils to assess the international situation correctly and to take positive measures to protect its citizens in the event of air raids. *Central Library Collection.*

Neighbours were positively encouraged to spy and inform on one another.

It was in an attempt to publicise their plight that the National Unemployed Workers Movement (NUWM) organized a series of marches and demonstrations throughout the country. On 1 October 1931, several hundred demonstrators gathered in the square in front of Salford Town Hall to protest at cuts in benefit and in a pitched battle with police, 12 demonstrators were arrested. A week later, nearly 5,000 men assembled at Ardwick Green for a march to Manchester Town Hall.

When informed by police that the intended route was 'provocative', fighting broke out. The following day, Manchester witnessed scenes reminiscent of the General Strike as police mounted guard on public buildings and Special Constables were mobilised on an unprecedented scale. The NUWM continued its

campaign throughout 1931 and into 1932, the worst disturbances occurring in Belfast where police opened fire on demonstrators in self-defence.

It was not until the Special Areas (Amendment) Act of 1937 that the possibilities for creating jobs on a large-scale was given a foothold. The Act incorporated proposals by Sir Malcolm Stewart that in return for opening a factory in a depressed area, a firm should be given tax, rent and rates incentives for a period of five years. Sir Malcolm's ideas led to the opening of a number of trading estates, where companies could lease ready-built premises with all services laid on.

Initially, the estates attracted only light industries but by the end of 1937, unemployment in the Special Areas had fallen by 155,000, although 67,000 of these had gone elsewhere in the search of work. But by now rearmament was beginning to take up industrial spare capacity and slowly but surely new jobs were being created.

The year 1937 also saw the resignation of Stanley Baldwin and the appointment of Neville Chamberlain as Prime Minister. Already nearly 70 years of age, Chamberlain had a lean hawkish look about him and always dressed in dark clothes and wing collars.

He had previously held Cabinet positions, having been Minister of Health in the Conservative Government of 1924-29, followed by a spell as Chancellor of the Exchequer in the National Government. In both posts Chamberlain had performed well and in the latter had done much to steer the economy out of recession.

As Prime Minister he proved to be obstinate, secretive, arrogant and impatient of criticism. He could be a natural dictator and ruled his cabinet with a rod of iron such as never seen before and only once since. He would, if necessary, ignore Parliament and avoid debate and on top of all this he utterly and totally distrusted the Foreign Office and had no hesitation in circumventing its officials in order to get his own way.

In matters of foreign policy Chamberlain had no love whatsoever for the Soviet Union and his dealings with the French, though inescapable, often proved to be far from cordial. Above all else, his hatred of war was without doubt passionate and sincere. He followed what he himself called a 'general scheme of appeasement' in the belief that it would solve Europe's problems and save us all from ever again having to experience the horror and the slaughter of World War One. But by 1937 the world was already heading inexorably towards an even greater and far bloodier confrontation.

The Rise of the Nazis
THE year 1923 was one of crisis for the Weimar Republic. Economic problems, including the collapse of the mark, runaway inflation and the occupation by French troops of the Ruhr over non-payment of reparations, led to a relatively unknown political opportunist named Adolf Hitler to attempt to overthrow the Berlin government.

The whole undertaking was doomed to failure. Hitler had overestimated the degree of support for his

Neville Chamberlain returns from Munich clutching the now famous piece of paper signed by Hitler. 'Peace for our time'.

National Socialist Nazi Party outside Bavaria. In fact the Nazis had no rating on a national level and were regarded merely as a paramilitary pressure group. Despite their failure, the Nazis credentials as a radical organization were established and Hitler's subsequent trial gave the party national publicity.

Hitler was still determined to gain power but realized that the way forward was through the ballot box, the gun could be saved for later.

By 1932, Germany had six million unemployed and rising. It was out of the misery of unemployment and low pay for those fortunate enough to be in work, that the class, ideological and racial doctrines of the Nazis grew and prospered. In July 1932 the Nazis polled 37.3 per cent of the vote in the General Election, which under the Republic's system of proportional representation gave them 230 seats in the Reichstag and made them the largest single party. Despite his known dislike of the Nazis and their politics, ageing President van Hindenburg had little choice but to offer Hitler the Chancellorship. It was January 1933.

Hitler was without doubt a charismatic figure and in his public speaking he could appeal to the collective conscious of people who had been humiliated in 1918 and by the Treaty of Versailles. Political opportunist he may well have been, but he was totally committed in his desire to see Germany once more established as the leading European power.

Hitler's first priority was to make his own position and authority unassailable. On 28 February 1933, a decree was issued under Article 48 of the Constitution suspending normal civil liberties. The following month came the 'Communist' plot culminating in the burning down of the Reichstag. Using Article 48, Hitler expelled all 83 Communist members of parliament and, by reaching an accord with the Centre

Party, achieved the majority required to pass the Enabling Law allowing him to issue legislation without having to seek the consent of parliament.

The stage was now set for the extension of Nazi control and influence over the whole range of Germany's institutions. However, the next stage in the process was hastened by the activities of the Sturmabteilung (SA), the Brown Shirt paramilitary wing of the party which had grown from around 100,000 storm troopers in 1930 to 4.5 million in 1934.

The SA, under its leader Ernst Röhm, wanted to take over control from the army. Fearing both an army-led counter coup and concerned that the SA was not only too powerful but becoming even more unruly and unpredictable than it already was, Hitler threw his lot in with the army. In return for eliminating the SA leadership in the 'Night of The Long Knives' on 30 June 1934, thereby reducing the SA to a subordinate role, Hitler acquired the direct backing of the army for his regime and most important of all, an oath of loyalty to the person of the Führer.

From 1934 onwards, Hitler pushed rearmament and the reinflation of the German economy to the limit. It was not a straightforward task. Germany was desperately short of foreign exchange which hampered the supply of imports, especially Swedish iron ore. The only raw material that Germany possessed in relative abundance was coal.

On 9 March 1935, Germany formally acknowledged for the first time that she possessed an air force (Luftwaffe) and a week later conscription was introduced to raise the strength of the army from 100,000 to 550,000 men. By the end of the year, the German navy had launched no less than 19 submarines, although these were coastal craft more suitable for training than for actual offensive operations.

In 1936, Hitler ordered German troops into the demilitarized Rhineland. Britain and France did nothing and Hitler gained the diplomatic initiative.

On 5 November 1937, the Führer met in secret session with his military advisers and told them of his desire to see an enlarged Reich by unification with Austria (Anschluss) and the annexation of Czechoslovakia. Any further territorial expansion would have to be accomplished by 1943, or at the latest by 1945 as it was estimated that by then Germany's military advantage would have worn away as the other powers re-armed.

Anschluss & Czechoslovakia

On 19 November 1937, Lord Halifax had visited the Führer in Bavaria to discuss the possibility of Germany obtaining colonies in Africa at the expense of Belgium and Portugal — for neither had been consulted — in return for an arms limitation treaty. Hitler, not surprisingly, was totally unimpressed. He was not interested in overseas colonies, yet, as they were often expensive to administer and difficult to hold in time of war. The empire which the Führer wished to create was in Europe — and Austria was to be the first acquisition.

On 12 February 1938, the Austrian Chancellor Kurt von Schuschnigg visited Hitler at Berchtesgaden. With typical Nazi panache, the route was lined somewhat menacingly with troops of Germany's 120,000 strong Austrian Legion. By the end of the meeting, von

27 July 1939. The first tribunals begin for conscientious objectors under the Military Training Act, 1939. Provision was made for conscientious objection on pacifist or political grounds. Unconditional exemption was granted to some, whilst others had to take specified work or non-combatant roles with the armed forces. Many objectors were to join bomb disposal units of their own accord, performing some of the most hazardous tasks of the war.

Schuschnigg had agreed to include Austrian Nazis in his Cabinet. The question of unification (*Anschluss*) was raised but no formal agreement reached. Hitler got the shock of his life a couple of weeks later when Schuschnigg announced that the question of unification would be decided by the people of Austria in a plebiscite. Fearing the vote could go against unification, the German High Command were ordered to improvise an invasion plan, troops making an unopposed crossing of the Austrian border on 11 March. The following day the country was annexed and Hitler drove in triumph through Vienna on the 13th.

Austria was completely integrated into the Reich, its economy developed and measures taken to end unemployment.

Hitler had anticipated, quite correctly, that neither Britain nor France would be prepared to use force over Austria since they had done nothing to stop him when he had ordered the re-occupation of the Rhineland. Neville Chamberlain's idea of purchasing peace through appeasement was that any settlement should involve concessions on both sides which would be honoured in perpetuity. Czechoslovakia was another matter.

Until the winter of 1937-38, German military planning had been purely defensive in nature although a directive of 27 June 1937 had provided for two possible deployments. Plan Red was to defeat a major French invasion in the west whilst holding a defensive line in the east against Czech or Polish intervention. Plan Green called for a pre-emptive strike against the Czechs whilst maintaining sufficient forces in the west to beat off the French. On 7 December 1937, Plan Green was given priority. Germany was moving on to a war footing.

Czechoslovakia was one of the new nations to emerge at the end of World War One. In the immediate post-war years, the Czech economy had flourished but the Wall Street Crash and the European banking crisis had had a devastating effect on her industries. With countries abandoning the gold standard and introducing import tariffs, the demand for Czech goods fell and unemployment rocketed, especially in the German-populated Sudetenland.

The continuing recession bought support for the Sudeten Nazi party, which, led by Konrad Henlein, won 44 seats in the 1935 election. With support from Berlin, the Sudetenlanders campaigned for self-determination and the campaign intensified following

a speech by Hitler on 20 February 1938, when he promised protection to all Germans living outside the Reich.

At the end of April the first of a series of Anglo-French meetings took place to consider the implications of German intentions towards Czechoslovakia. British policy toward the Czechs was both ill-informed and unsympathetic. The French, on the other hand, were bound by treaty to aid the Czechs if they were attacked but the French army was geared towards defensive rather than offensive operations and, in any case, both the French Press and public opinion were strongly pacifist.

Also, the French feared that in the event of a shooting war they would be without British support. Outwardly the Anglo-French conversations were portrayed as the working out of a joint policy. Behind the scenes, both governments had decided to abandon the Czechs to their fate but a public announcement to that effect would have been political suicide. At all costs the Czechs had to be deserted in a way that would preserve French honour.

During May, Henlein visited London and reported

At 4.40am on 1 September 1939, the German battleship *Schleswig-Holstein* began a close-range bombardment of Polish fortifications at Westerplatte near Danzig. An hour later, German armoured formations crossed the frontier and the Luftwaffe launched air-strikes against Warsaw, Cracow and other cities.

back to Berlin that the British Government were sympathetic to the Sudeten cause. In any case Chamberlain saw no benefit to Great Britain in an independent Czechoslovakia and he shared Hitler's dislike of the Czech alliances with France and the Soviet Union. Chamberlain's views were also influenced by the Dominions, who had little, if any, sympathy for a British guarantee.

On 20 May, two days before the Czech municipal elections, the Führer ordered General Keitel to dust off Plan Green just in case the French decided to intervene. Any military action against the Czechs had to be launched quickly so as to deny Britain and France any time to react. Within days German troops were massing along the Czech border.

With 35 divisions, excellent fortifications and tanks far superior to anything the Germans had, the Czech army was certainly capable of giving a good account of itself. The German army, however, had expanded so rapidly that many units were untrained and there was a serious shortage of officers and NCOs. There was only six weeks supply of munitions and fuel reserves stood at only 25 per cent of the mobilization requirement.

In the air the Luftwaffe was in no fit state to get involved in a war of attrition. The force was in the middle of a transition phase caused by new generations of fighters and bombers being introduced from 1936 onwards. On 1 August 1938 the operational strength of the Luftwaffe stood at 49 per cent of the bomber force and 70 per cent for the fighter arm. The whole of the Luftwaffe was only 57 per cent operational and only with drastic reductions in flying hours and training schedules could the force be brought up to a respectable in-commission rate — but that would take at least eight weeks. To add to the problems, the reserves of some essential aircraft lubricants stood at only 6 per cent of mobilization requirements.

The German strength, without any doubt, was their propaganda machine. Throughout the summer, a superbly orchestrated campaign gave the impression that Germany's military capability was far greater than it actually was. Visiting dignitaries were taken on whistle-stop tours of Luftwaffe bases and shown the might of the German air force. What they were not privy to was the fact that some of the squadrons of modern combat aircraft were being flown from one airfield to another in order to beef up the numbers.

On 4 September, the Czech Government finally cracked. Fearing civil war and unable to act without French, Russian or British support, President Benes agreed to all Sudeten demands. Nine days later, Hitler demanded that the Sudetenland be granted self-determination. Within hours rioting had broken out and martial law declared, Henlein fleeing to Berlin. British diplomatic moves at this stage consisted of attempting to deter the Germans with hints of probable intervention, whilst at the same time discouraging the Czechs from fighting with less than subtle hints of non-intervention. Hitler, sensing a bluff, demanded the annexation of the Sudetenland.

The French panicked and abdicated all initiatives to Britain. Daladier begged Chamberlain to do something — anything — to get France off the hook of having to honour her treaty obligations. Chamberlain flew to Bechtesgaden to see Herr Hitler. During their three-hour meeting, Hitler made it quite plain that unless Britain accepted Germany's claims there was little point in talking. Chamberlain was in no position to negotiate an on-the-spot agreement but offered to consult with the Cabinet if Germany, in the meantime, would refrain from opening hostilities. Hitler agreed.

Chamberlain was now convinced that the only viable course of action open was the ceding of the Sudetenland to Germany. Daladier came to London and agreed to a plan whereby Germany would be allowed to annex all Czech territory containing a majority German population. The Czechs, now facing the loss of even more territory than previously thought, found the proposals unacceptable even though they were left in no doubt whatsoever that Britain would not fight and France would ignore her treaty obligations.

On 22 September, Chamberlain met Hitler at Godesberg. Sensing victory the Führer upped the price of peace by insisting that Czech forces withdraw from the German areas but that they leave all military installations intact. He also demanded plebiscites to be held in all other areas of Czechoslovakia which had a German minority. Chamberlain, well aware that British public opinion was hardening against further concessions, flew back to London where he held a series of crisis meetings with the Cabinet and later the French.

Lord Halifax urged the Prime Minister to make one last effort to reach an agreement with Hitler. The outcome was that Sir Horace Wilson was to deliver to Hitler a personal letter appealing to him to allow the details of any settlement to be overseen by an international committee of Czech, German and British officials. If Hitler refused, Wilson was to tell him that France would stand by the Czechs and Britain would stand by France.

As the situation deteriorated, air-raid trenches were dug in public parks and what few anti-aircraft guns there were were trundled into positions around London. On the morning of 26 September, British and French officials discussed the military implications of the crisis and war was considered a viable option. Later in the day, Chamberlain told the Cabinet that Britain would stand by France in the event of war. Hitler had lost his chance of ordering a pre-emptive strike. A conference was hurriedly arranged.

On the 29th as Chamberlain flew to Munich, Britain was on the verge of panic as many people hoarded food, fuel and petrol whilst others took off for remote areas unlikely to be bombed. Plans were announced for the evacuation of nearly two million people from London and gas masks were issued to all civilians except babies — there weren't any for the youngest members of the population.

Munich opened with neither Czechoslovakia nor the Soviet Union represented. In reality the conference was little more than a sham, for despite the sabre rattling Chamberlain was still determined to follow the path of appeasement. Chamberlain and Hitler signed, upon the initiative of the former, a declaration that the two countries would in future settle any sources of difference by negotiation. Hitler was persuaded to agree to a progressive occupation of the Sudetenland and a commission to determine the status of the remaining areas with predominantly German populations.

The result of Munich was that Hitler had gained everything he had wanted and at the same time had destroyed France's military credibility. Also, he had inflicted a diplomatic defeat upon Great Britain and left Poland and the Soviet Union isolated in an uncertain world.

Chamberlain had, however, averted war. He came home to an albeit brief hero's welcome. The British Press applauded him but at the same time voiced concern over the future. Only one member of the Government, Duff Cooper, had the courage to resign in protest at the betrayal of the Czechs, although Winston Churchill and a number of other Conservative MPs abstained when the Commons voted on the final agreement.

4th SEPTEMBER, 1939

GOLD MUST BE SOLD TO THE TREASURY

If you have any gold coins you must take it to the bank and sell it to the Treasury. Luxury imports, including motor-cars, clothing and perfumery, are banned.

These regulations were issued last night.

Residents in Britain must offer foreign securities and bullion, as well as gold coin, to their bankers.

Foreign exchange to be offered for sale includes currencies named by the Treasury from time to time. Those already named include:—

U.S. dollars, Guilders, Canadian dollars, Argentine pesos, Belgas, Swedish crowns, Swiss francs, Norwegian crowns and French francs.

Persons may apply through their bankers for permission to retain gold and foreign exchange required to meet contracts, made before the coming into force of these regulations, which provide for payments in gold or foreign exchange, for meeting the reasonable requirements of trade or business, or for reasonable travelling or other personal expenses.

Prices to be paid for gold and foreign exchange offered for sale are to be determined by the Treasury, and may be ascertained by inquiry at any bank.

The public should continue to transact business in foreign exchange and gold through the agency of their bankers.

Applications for exchange must be made on the appropriate form, and satisfactory evidence in regard to the transaction proposed must be produced in all cases.

Export of banknotes, gold, securities or foreign currency is prohibited except with permission.

Traders Must Insure

The order issued by the Board of Trade bans the imports, except under licence, of luxuries and goods of which there are sufficient home supplies.

This will conserve exchange for the additional purchases of other products required in war time.

The main categories of goods covered by the order are pottery and glass, cutlery, clocks and watches, textile goods and apparel (including footwear), certain chemicals and paints, soap, office machinery (including typewriters), motor-cars, musical instruments, perfumery and toilet requisites, toys and games and luxury foodstuffs.

Traders in Britain who sell goods liable to King's enemy risks must insure them under the War Risks Insurance Act.

This is part of a scheme which the Board of Trade has put into operation.

Liability of the Board as insurers will be determined by a policy of insurance issued in a form prescribed in the schedule of the War Risks (Commodity Insurance) (No. 1) Order.

Insurance is compulsory except where the value of a person's insurable goods does not exceed £1,000.

BILLETS BY ORDER, IF—

A FEW householders who have so far been unwilling to receive evacuees are asked not to force the Government to exercise compulsion.

Making this appeal yesterday, Sir Warren Fisher, the North-West Regional Commissioner, pointed out:

"It is not possible at present to say how long the billets will last.

"But all must be prepared for danger and hardship, and will be lucky if it takes no worse a form than receiving strangers into one's house.

"No war can be won under modern conditions unless the essential work of the towns can be continued in spite of air raids. This will be easier if the townspeople in dangerous areas can be relieved of anxiety for their young children.

"It is also of vital importance to preserve the lives of children, who will be the citizens of the next generation, so that householders in safer districts must take them in.

"Parliament has given powers to billet them compulsorily in the reception areas, and the Government is determined to use those powers if necessary."

HITLER BLAMES BRITAIN

HITLER, in messages to his Army of the West and to the German people yesterday, blamed Britain for the war.

He claimed that the Poles had "attacked" Germany, and that he was fighting to "establish peace." He added that he was on the way to the Eastern Front.

To his troops on the Western Front he said (according to the German News Agency, quoted by Reuter):—

"The British Government, driven on by those warmongers whom we knew in the last war, has resolved to let fall its mask and to proclaim war on a threadbare pretext.

"For months it (the British Government) has supported the Polish attacks against the lives and security of fellow-Germans, and the rape of the Free City of Danzig," continued Hitler.

"In a Few Months"

"Now that Poland, with the consciousness of this protection, has undertaken acts of aggression against Reich territory, I have determined to blow up this ring which has been laid round Germany.

"Sections of the German Army in the East have now, for two days, in response to Polish attacks, been fighting for the establishment of a peace which shall assure life and freedom to the German people.

"If you do your duty, the battle in the East will have reached its successful conclusion in a few months, and then the power of the whole Nazi State stands behind you.

"As an old soldier of the world war, and as your supreme commander, I am going, with confidence in you, to the Army on the East."

"Unity or—" Threat

To the German people Hitler said the English "encirclement" policy was resumed when the "peaceful" revision of the Versailles Treaty seemed to be succeeding.

To this he added: "The same lying inciters appeared as in 1914."

Claiming that "as long as the German people was united it has never been conquered," Hitler uttered this threat:—

"Whoever offends against this unity need expect nothing else than annihilation as an enemy of the nation."

DUKE TAKES UP NAVAL POST

The Admiralty announces that Rear-Admiral His Royal Highness the Duke of Kent has taken up his war appointment.

Immediately after Mr. Chamberlain's dramatic broadcast to the nation, the Government yesterday announced a number of precautionary measures to prevent people crowding together and so increasing the casualty risks from air raids.

Instructions were given for the closing of all places of entertainment until further notice. In the light of experience it may be possible to open cinemas and theatres in some areas later. Included in the closure orders are indoor and outdoor sports gatherings where large numbers of people might be expected to congregate.

The following advice is given:—

Keep off the streets as much as possible; to expose yourself unnecessarily adds to your danger.

Carry your gas mask with you always.

Make sure every member of your household have on them their names and addresses clearly written. Do this on an envelope or luggage label and not on an odd piece of paper which may be lost.

Sew a label on children's clothing so that they cannot pull it off.

People are requested not to crowd together unnecessarily in any circumstances.

Churches and other places of public worship will not be closed.

All day schools in evacuation and neutral areas in England, Wales and Scotland are to be closed for lessons for at least a week from yesterday.

In the reception areas schools will be opened as soon as evacuation is complete.

Cinemas, Theatres Close to Cut Risks

PETROL IS RATIONED

PETROL rationing will be introduced, as from September 16. This was announced last night by the Secretary for Mines. Information as to how the public can secure their ration books will be announced to-day.

There are very substantial stocks of petrol in the country, but in the national interests the best use must be made of these supplies.

Petrol distributors have arranged to pool all their resources and, after the individual brands still in stock at garages and service stations have been sold by them at prices now ruling, one grade only of motor spirit will be supplied to the public.

This spirit will be called "Pool" motor spirit, and will be on sale, ex-pump, in England and Wales at 1s. 6d. a gallon.

Appeal to Owners

No change will be made in the price for the next fourteen days at least. From to-day no further supplies of individual brands to be made at garages and service stations.

For at least the same period of fourteen days there will be no change in yesterday's bulk prices to those commercial concerns who receive their supplies direct.

Owners and drivers of commercial vehicles are particularly asked to note that it will no longer be possibly to allow commercial vehicles to call at petrol companies' depots for supplies. The Government appeal to all owners of motor vehicles to use them only for essential purposes.

BANKS ARE SHUT TO-DAY

TO-DAY has been declared a limited Bank Holiday, affecting only banks. The arrangement applies to the Post Office Savings Bank and other savings banks.

This day will be used by the banks to complete their measures for adapting themselves to the emergency, and to-morrow morning the banks will be open for business.

The Treasury, in conjunction with the Bank of England, have taken all the steps needed to ensure that the banks (including the Post Office Savings Bank and other savings banks) will be amply supplied with currency.

Postal orders will be legal tender for the present, and Scottish and Northern Ireland banknotes will be legal tender in Scotland and Northern Ireland respectively.

AIR MAIL CURTAILED

Empire air mail services are from to-day restricted to two services weekly in each direction between the United Kingdom and Sydney and one weekly in each direction between the United Kingdom and Durban and between the United Kingdom and Kisumu.

Corresponding modifications will be made in the overseas connecting services operated by Imperial Airways.

Present arrangements under which first-class mail to certain countries is forwarded by Empire Air Mail services without surcharge will be suspended, and a surcharge will be imposed on all mail from the United Kingdom carried by air on the Empire routes.

Day-old Babies Leave

Three babies born only the previous day were among three trainloads of evacuees from London yesterday.

Accompanied by their mothers, they were driven in an ambulance from the station to a nursing home which has been taken over as a maternity home.

U.S. REFUGEES LEAVE LONDON

BETWEEN two and three thousand American refugees left London last night. Many of them were destitute.

An American Embassy official said it might take ten days before sufficient ships to evacuate these people will have put in.

Mr. Joseph Kennedy, American Ambassador, has requested all American and other neutral steamship lines to provide all available ships, including freighters and tankers, for evacuation.

WARNINGS TO SHIPPING

The Board of Trade announces: "Shipping is hereby warned that all traffic proceeding through the Dover Straits must proceed through the Downs. Ships disregarding this warning do so at their own peril."

The Admiralty give notice that vessels entering the Firth of Forth must pass to the northward of Bass Rock. Vessels proceeding to the southward of Bass Rock will do so at their own peril.

Poland

ON 24 March 1939, Britain and France agreed to resist any German aggression against Belgium, Holland and Switzerland. A week later, Britain said that she would stand by France in guaranteeing Poland's frontiers. On 3 and 11 April, the Führer issued directives to the Wehrmacht to prepare for the invasion of Poland.

Poland's affairs were dominated by her relations with her neighbours, none of whom were too pleased with the frontiers settled upon her by the Treaty of Versailles. By the end of 1921, the infant Polish Republic had fought no less than six wars and had inflicted a heavy defeat upon the Russians. But the experience of being left to fight the Soviet Union single-handed, despite mutual-aid treaties with Britain and France, permanently damaged relations with London and Paris.

On 25 January 1932, Poland signed a non-aggression pact with Russia, concluding a similar ten-year agreement with Germany on 26 January 1934.

The real threat to Poland came after the Nazi Party had gained control of the free city of Danzig. There is evidence to suggest that the Poles had considered launching an all-out preventive war against Germany but had refrained from doing so because Britain and France had refused to get involved. Hitler, inspired by the apparent inability of the Western Powers to get their act together and do anything to stop him, decided that the time had come for Danzig to be returned to the Reich. In return for Danzig and access across Polish territory, Hitler offered the Poles a guarantee of their frontiers. The Poles refused to negotiate.

On 20 August 1939, the world was stunned by the news that the Soviet Union and Nazi Germany had signed a trade agreement. Further shocks were in store for the Western Allies and the United States just three days later, when Russia and Germany signed a non-aggression pact undertaking not to attack each other and to remain neutral if either attacked a third power. There was also a second, secret agreement in which Russia would get Estonia and Latvia whilst Germany would take Lithuania and Vilna. Poland was to be divided between them.

With Hitler demanding the annexation of Danzig, Britain requested American help in the growing Polish crisis. Unfortunately, the United States ambassador to London, Joseph Kennedy, proved little better than useless in that his reports on the situation bordered on hysteria. He also got the basic plot wrong by informing Washington that Britain wanted Poland forced into unilateral concessions with Germany. In fact, what Chamberlain wanted was for the Poles to state their willingness to negotiate in order to put Hitler in the wrong should he attack. On the other hand, if Hitler agreed to talks, then there was a chance that the Poles could drag the proceedings out until the onset of the winter rains when an invasion would become virtually impossible.

Dawn on the 26 August had been the time set by Hitler to unleash the Wehrmacht against Poland, but on the evening of the 25th, all orders were suddenly cancelled when the Italian dictator, Benito Mussolini, dropped something of a bombshell on the Führer by informing him that Italy was in no fit state to honour her treaty obligations to Germany without massive military and material aid.

Italy had drawn close to Germany from 1936 onwards and although Mussolini possessed wide-ranging powers and the Fascists were the only political party, he had to take into account the views of the Vatican City, the Church in Italy and the monarchy that Italy did not possess the economic, political and military infrastructure to wage a war concurrently with Germany.

On the 25th, Hitler met with Sir Neville Henderson, the British ambassador to Berlin, and told him that Germany desired a settlement with Britain and that he, Hitler, was prepared to guarantee the British Empire and would approach London with an offer once the Polish question had been settled.

There followed three days of intense diplomatic and political activity. The Cabinet met to consider the implications of Hitler's message. Britain warned Germany against resorting to force and that Britain would honour her obligations to the Poles. On the evening of the 28th, Hitler took up the diplomatic initiative by asking Henderson 'whether England would be willing to accept an alliance with Germany.' The ambassador exceeded his instructions and replied that, 'speaking personally', he did not exclude the possibility provided that 'the development of events justified it'.

Hitler's moderate tone raised hopes in London where unfortunately it was interpreted as a sign that the Führer was weakening in his resolve due to Germany's isolated position and that if brought to the negotiating table, he would buckle and give in. However, Henderson's response to offers of what might be interpreted as an Anglo-German military alliance was political dynamite, which if leaked, would wreck Anglo-American relations. Henderson was warned against making such personal statements in the future.

On the evening of the 29th, Hitler announced his willingness to talk, provided that a Polish emissary arrived in Berlin by noon the following day. He denied that this was an ultimatum, although he still hoped to divide London and Warsaw. He was convinced that Chamberlain could be tempted into an alliance and that two interesting scenarios would then arise.

Firstly, the Poles might refuse to talk in which case the British would be justified in revoking their treaty obligations. Secondly, if a Polish emissary did arrive, the talks could always break down and Chamberlain might refuse to fight on the grounds that the Poles had provoked war. Chamberlain, to his credit, had no intention of being drawn into a trap. He informed the Cabinet that the demand for a Polish emissary was unacceptable and that any Anglo-German agreement depended upon a just settlement for Poland backed by international guarantees.

At 4pm on the 31st, Hitler decided that he could delay no longer and ordered the Wehrmacht to attack the following morning.

At around 8pm, Sturmban Führer Alfred Navjocks led an attack on a German radio station at Gleiwitz in Upper Silesia. His force included a dozen convicted criminals dressed in Polish uniforms, who were promised a reprieve in return for their co-operation. Having forced their way into the station, The 'Poles' fired a few pistol shots and broadcast a patriotic announcement. Once outside they were summarily executed and their bodies left for the local police to find. Before the night was out, Eastern Europe was hearing reports of a Polish attack upon the Third Reich.

At 4.40am on 1 September, the German battleship *Schleswig-Holstein*, which was moored in the port of Danzig on a friendship visit, opened fire at close-range on the Polish fortifications at Westerplatte. An hour later, German armour crossed the frontier and the Luftwaffe launched air-raids against Warsaw, Lódź, Czestochowa, Cracow and Poznán. With only 159 fighter planes to defend the entire Polish air space, the Polish Air Force soon lost irreplaceable aircraft and pilots and its strength was whittled away.

The Polish army, with a strength on paper of 40 divisions, was overwhelmed in many sectors before reserves could be fully mobilized. It was also having to contend with the fact than many dispositions had been made for political rather than sound military reasons, resulting in units attempting to defend the indefensible.

The French were partially to blame. They delayed issuing a statement of intent as Daladier was still attempting to find a peaceful solution which in turn induced the Poles into delaying mobilization with the result that 25 per cent of the army never reached the front.

Britain and France, using Mussolini as an intermediary, said that they were still willing to negotiate if German troops were withdrawn, but Hitler, anticipating a short sharp war of no more than two weeks, rejected the proposal.

The War Office issued instructions to the Regular Army and all Territorial Army units that general mobilization had been proclaimed and that all troops should report to their depots. Under the Defence Regulations, the black-out came into force at sunset on 1 September. It would last for 2,061 consecutive nights. On the first night, however, Coventry was totally blacked out, save for the traffic-lights which someone forgot to switch off.

On Saturday 2 September, the evacuation of school children, toddlers, expectant mums and the disabled was into its second day, although the numbers actually leaving varied from one place to another. From Sheffield, for instance, 20 LNER evacuation trains took youngsters to Newark, Bingham, Ruddington and Kimberley but the second train to reach Newark carried only 266 children, despite having places for 840.

On the international scene, Denmark, Sweden, Finland, Iceland, Norway, Latvia and Estonia declared their neutrality. Italy said that she would not take any initiative in military operations and Japan declared that the German-Soviet non-aggression pact exempted her from supporting Germany in the event of war.

At 7.30pm, Neville Chamberlain addressed the Commons. Members of both sides had expected to be told that an ultimatum had been delivered to Berlin. Instead they were treated to the news that there was still the possibility of a conference if Hitler withdrew his troops. Chamberlain sat down before a silent House, no cheers, no applause, nothing. The acting Labour leader, Arthur Greenwood, rose to his feet and, encouraged by members of all parties, spoke: "Every minutes delay," he said, "now means loss of life, imperilling our national interests . . .I wonder how long we are prepared to vacillate?"

That night, ministers Hore-Belisha, Anderson, Colville, de la Warr, Dorman-Smith, Stanley, Wallace and Elliott met with Sir John Simon and plotted. Later, Sir Simon and his co-conspirators called on the Prime Minister and told him bluntly that the Cabinet would no longer co-operate with him until war was declared. At last Chamberlain spoke, "Right, gentlemen, this means war." Almost simultaneously there was tremendous clap of thunder as a storm of almost Biblical proportions rolled over Central London. At 11pm, the Cabinet met in emergency session.

At 9am on Sunday 3 September, an ultimatum was delivered to Berlin. It expired two hours later without reply and at 11.15am, Chamberlain spoke to the nation on the radio.

At 11.27am, the air-raid sirens sounded over London and people made their way in uneasy anticipation to the shelters. A few minutes later, the all-clear sounded. It had been a false alarm caused by a single French aircraft, but two formations of RAF fighter planes had been scrambled from different air fields into the skies over the Thames, where they engaged each other in earnest. Two planes were shot down and one pilot killed.

The Home Front

ON 27 September 1939, Sir John Simon placed his Emergency War Budget before the House of Commons. Petrol was the first commodity to be rationed but those who needed cars for their work — such as country doctors — were to receive supplementary supplies. Whisky duty was increased and expected to bring in £3.5 million (the cost of 11 destroyers for the Royal Navy) in a full year, and the basic duty on tobacco was increased from 11s 6d to 13s 6d per pound, adding 1½d per ounce on the shop price. Sugar duty was also increased which led to higher prices in the shops for tinned fruit as well as jam, marmalade, syrup and sweetened milk.

The rationing of basic food stuffs was introduced in January 1940. The weekly allowance per person included 2oz tea (none for the under-fives), 2oz butter, 4oz sugar, 2oz sweets, 2oz of fats and 4oz margarine. Extra cheese was available to those workers who had no canteen facilities and a special ration was allowed for vegetarians on the condition that they surrendered their meat coupons. Meat rations were set at 6oz per head per day, although this was prime cuts only; people could buy cheaper cuts to the value of 6oz of prime beef, mutton or pork.

When it was announced the 1940 Budget was expected to raise the largest sum in taxation in one year in British history. Sir John spoke for two hours and seven minutes in which he revealed that estimated expenditure for the coming year at £2,667,000,000, of which he expected to raise £1,234,000,000 from revenue. Income Tax was raised from 7s to 7s 6d in the pound and surtax was levied on those whose incomes exceeded £1,500 a year. The price of beer was increased by one penny a pint, whisky by 1s 9d a bottle to 16s, tobacco duty by 3d an ounce and matches by a halfpenny per box. Postal charges for inland letters went up by a penny and inland telephone calls by 15 per cent.

That year the points system was introduced for clothing and tinned meats. Tinned salmon, crab, oranges, pineapples and the like were not officially rationed, as imports virtually ceased anyway. Another commodity to disappear was bananas. The official Ministry of Food statement said: "Bananas are a bulky cargo compared with other foods. Oranges, for instance, have far greater vitamin value than bananas and occupy far less space. We want to use ships for more important cargoes than bananas."

The great banana ban threw a thousand people out of work in Britain and seriously affected the economy of Jamaica, whose banana trade represented more than half of the island's total exports. Before the war, the UK imported 45 million a week; wartime restrictions before the ban had reduced this to about 28 million. And what of the oranges mentioned by the Ministry of Food? They also became scarce. Sporadic deliveries, usually from South Africa, were reserved for the young and for mothers with an RB2 ration book.

In February 1942, Sir Stafford Cripps, officially introduced austerity to the UK: "Personal extravagance must be eliminated altogether." There was to be no petrol for pleasure motoring, a reduction in the

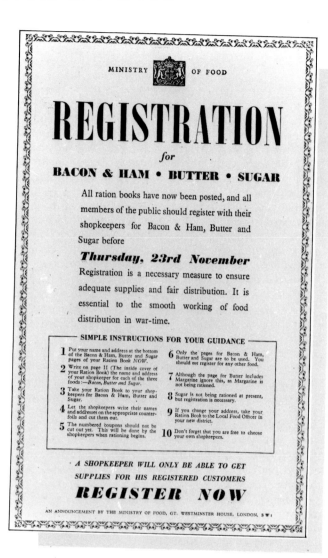

clothing ration was introduced and sporting events were curtailed.

Silk stockings became a thing of the past, imports falling from 33 million pairs in 1938 to only 718,000 pairs during 1944. Women resorted to painting their legs with gravy browning whilst praying that it did not rain. Others, in desperation, resorted to silk stocking snatching, risking fines and up to 28 days' imprisonment if caught.

Entertainment and sport continued, albeit modified throughout the war. BBC television had closed for the duration but few people in 1939 could afford the luxury of owning a set. However, nine out of ten homes had a radio and most people between the ages of 16 and 35 went to the cinema at least once a week.

On 8 September 1939, BBC radio was reorganized, a number of programmes being cancelled and others updated. A BBC repertory company was formed with a nucleus of 36 actors and actresses including D.A.Clarke-Smith, Carleton Hobbs, Thea Holme, Philip Wade and Patric Curwen. The variety department announced that it would retain the services of such people as Tommy Handley, Leonard Henry and Doris Arnold. Seventy-five members of the BBC Symphony Orchestra were also to be retained.

On 16 September 1939, Arthur Askey and Richard

'Stinker' Murdoch and the 'Bagwashers' returned with a new series of *Bandwagon*. Three days later the BBC broadcast the first of what was probably their most famous comedy programme of the war — *ITMA*.

A pilot series of four programmes had been transmitted the previous July. Tommy Handley (*It's that Man Again*) was the host, the programme format having been changed so that the series could lampoon the war in Europe in general and British Civil Service and the Nazi heirachy in particular. Handley played the Minister of Aggravation and Mysteries, Dorothy Summers was Mrs Mopp ("Can I do you now Sir?"). Other characters were played by Fred Yule ('Chief Bigga Banga'), Dino Galvani ('Signor So-So'), Sydney Keith ('Sam Scram') and Jack Train ('Colonel Chinstrap').

Each programme included a send up of Radio Luxembourg which had ceased transmitting. Maurice Denham announced, "This is Radio Fakenburg," and Sam Costa sang spoof commercials. The programme went out on Thursday nights and was repeated for the benefit of British Forces overseas. Of *ITMA* it was once said by a gentleman of the Royal Household that, "If the war were to end between 8.30 and 9.00 on a Thursday night, none of the Household would dare tell the King until *ITMA* has finished."

Other popular shows included Rob Wilton in *Nether Backwash*, Jack Warner in *Garrison Theatre*, and Ben Lyon and Bebe Daniels in *Life with the Lyons* and *Hi Gang!* Broadcast twice daily was *Music While You Work* and on most lunchtimes *Workers' Playtime* came from a factory 'somewhere in England'.

Dance band music filled much of the air time, some of the favourites being Billy Cotton, Joe Loss, Jack Hylton and Henry Hall. When the American Forces

Network was established, British listeners were treated to the big band sounds of Tommy Dorsey, Glenn Miller; jazz from Benny Carter; the singing talents of Ella Fitzgerald and a new singing phenomenon named Frank Sinatra. American comedians such as Jack Benny, Bob Hope and Red Skelton proved to be popular with British audiences.

Of all the American influences in the world of entertainment, it is probably the music of Glenn Miller that has since become synonymous with the war. Miller's hits included *Moonlight Serenade, Tuxedo Junction, In The Mood, Pennsylvania Six-Five Thousand* and *Little Brown Jug,* and he surprised many Americans by enlisting in the United States Army.

Given the responsibility of organizing various service bands, Miller came to England in June 1944. On 15 December, he boarded a single-engined C-64 Norseman at Bedford aerodrome for a flight to Paris where the Miller Band was scheduled to give a concert due to be broadcast live back to America. The plane took off into the mist and was never seen again. Ten days later, on Christmas Day, Glenn Miller was reported as missing in action.

Cinemas and theatres had been closed as an air-raid precaution on 3 September 1939 but reopened two weeks later to capacity audiences. Some of the films doing the rounds then were *The Prince and The Pauper* starring Errol Flynn, *The Show Goes On* (Gracie Fields), *White Banners* (Claude Rains and Fay Bainter), *The Lady Vanishes* (Margaret Lockwood and Michael Redgrave) and young Mickey Rooney in *Huckleberry Finn*.

In October 1939, the Football League was reorganized on a regional basis, Hull City playing in the North-East Regional League with Darlington, Hartlepools United, Leeds United, York City, Huddersfield Town, both Bradford clubs, Middlesbrough, Newcastle United and Halifax Town.

The Tigers finished seventh after an uninspiring season in which they had had to call on the services of 27 players. The 11-1 thrashing they had meted out to Carlisle United on 14 January 1939 must have belonged to another world. After playing in the 1940-41 North Regional League, in which the Tigers finished third from bottom as positions were decided on goal-average alone, the decision was taken to stop playing until the end of the war.

In this season no less than 38 players had been used for 23 games that had included an eight-goal drubbing by Middlesbrough. The Anlaby Road ground was handed over to the Home Guard and was also used as a repair depot for armoured vehicles. When Hull City began their peacetime campaign in 1946 it would be in the brand new stadium of Boothferry Park.

Rugby continued, the strict Union-League segregation disappearing as amateurs and professionals alike joined forces in scratch sides. Cricket also carried on, although The Oval was taken over by the Army, who not only sank concrete posts into the hallowed turf but erected huts and buildings to transform the ground into a prisoner-of-war camp which, as it turned out, was never used.

Yorkshire ended 1939 as County Champions once more. The last county game played at Hull before the war resulted in victory over Leicestershire by an

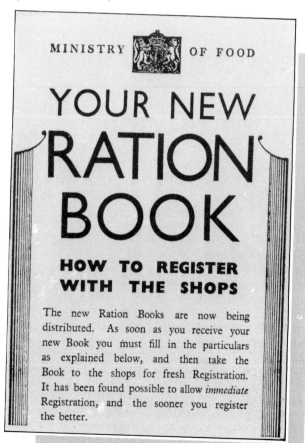

MINISTRY [crest] OF FOOD

YOUR NEW
RATION
BOOK

HOW TO REGISTER
WITH THE SHOPS

The new Ration Books are now being distributed. As soon as you receive your new Book you must fill in the particulars as explained below, and then take the Book to the shops for fresh Registration. It has been found possible to allow *immediate* Registration, and the sooner you register the better.

Registering for rations, 24 November 1939.

innings and 30 runs in early June 1939. In Yorkshire's 500 for 7 declared, the great Herbert Sutcliffe scored 234 not out.

The West Indian tourists cut short their trip and sailed for home as war clouds gathered and the MCC's winter tour to India was cancelled. For 1940 the three-day county matches were replaced with one-day games and teams fielding scratch sides. A spectator sport later reintroduced by the Americans was baseball. A baseball league had existed in England in the latter quarter of the nineteenth century — hence the Baseball Ground where Derby County FC play — but the game never really caught on in Britain, although the Hull area has remained one of its few strongholds. During the war baseball became a Saturday evening event in summer, complete with cheer leaders, running commentary and all the razzamataz.

But if sport survived, for many people holidays at the seaside became a thing of the past. The emphasis was on stay-at-home holidays or walking or cycling, as transport was needed for essential war purposes. The Railway Executive Committee actively discouraged people from using trains unless their journey was absolutely necessary. In any case, all passenger trains were restricted to a maximum speed of 60mph in the interests of fuel economy. This meant that the London-Edinburgh express took nearly eight and a half hours to complete the journey and passengers had to take their own food and drink as there were no longer any restaurant cars in service.

At the beginning of 1945, the weekly basic ration was 4oz bacon, 2oz tea, 8oz sugar, 8oz fat, 3oz cheese, meat to the value of 1s 2d (about a pound in weight), and two pints of milk. In March, the milk ration was increased by an extra half-pint per person per week but in May the bacon and lard rations were reduced by 1oz and the points available for canned meats reduced from 24 to 20. The cuts proved temporary and were restored the following October.

The astonishing fact is that the health of the nation as a whole improved during the war. School meals were provided, expectant mothers were allowed to go to the front of queues for rations, and, together with young children, were allowed extra milk, orange juice, eggs, cod-liver oil and vitamins. Factory workers benefited from works canteens and local authorities set up British Restaurants to serve inexpensive meals to the general public. By law British Restaurants were forbidden to charge more than 5s for a meal.

On top of this there was the *Dig For Victory* campaign. Begun at the outbreak of the war, the aim was for every family to have its own allotment or garden where they could grow produce to supplement their rations. If a man did not have an allotment, the local authorities would provide one, and although allotments were usually to be found on either

previously unused, waste or derelict land, nothing was sacred. In Manchester, for instance, Piccadilly Circus disappeared under carrots and cabbage.

Another source of extra supplies came from keeping hens or perhaps a pig or two, the latter developing into a craze involving hundreds of thousands of households fattening their family pet on the kitchen waste; the former became business orientated with domestic poultry keepers supplying a quarter of the country's fresh eggs by the end of 1943.

Another source of supplies was the 'Black Market', the Arthur English world of trilby and kipper tie, where a bottle of whisky sold at £5 and sugar at 1s. Clothing coupons fetched 2s to 5s each and parachute silk could be readily obtained to be transformed into bridal wear or lingerie. For the motoring fraternity, Black Market petrol traded at around 4s a gallon.

Petrol rationing was introduced only three weeks after the start of the war, but in February 1942, Sir Stafford Cripps, the Leader of the House of Commons and Lord Privy Seal, announced that not only was the clothing ration to be cut and sporting events curtailed, but also that petrol for 'pleasure motoring' would be stopped. Cripps would henceforce be for ever associated with austerity and utility.

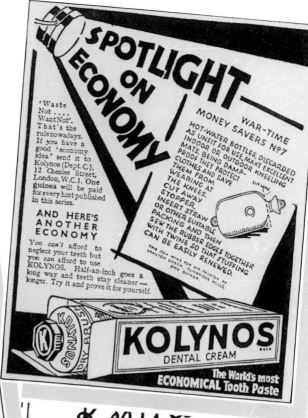
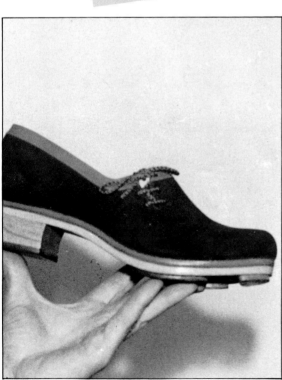

Wood-soled shoes make the newspapers in January 1943. The sole and heel were made of birch or poplar and the toe curved up to allow for the heel-toe action in walking. Leather treads, which had to be renewed before they were completely worn down, were nailed to the wooden side.

The very latest in Utility dresses in May 1942. *Left:* Short-sleeved spring dress in light blue wool with navy contrast. *Centre:* short-sleeved spring dress in navy and white check Scottish tweed. *Right:* Summer tunic in brown and white moygashel rayon.

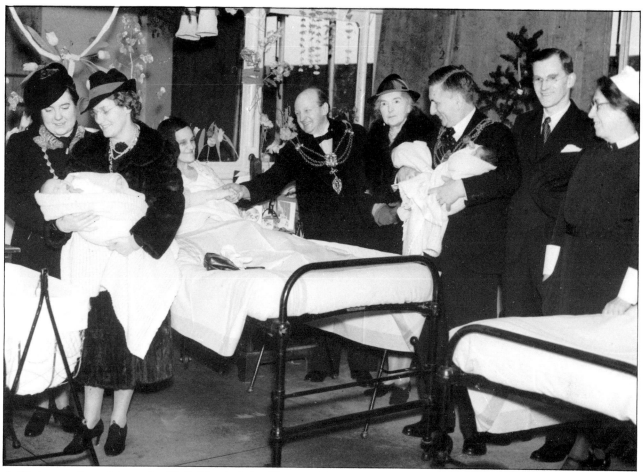

A Christmas Day visit to the Hull Hospital for Women by the Lord Mayor, Councillor Sydney Smith, 25 December 1940.

Members of the Home Guard help out at a Christmas dinner for underprivileged children held at the Queen's Hall, 1940.

Staying with the Christmas
theme, guests and helpers
pose for the camera at the
Young People's Ball, 27
December 1940.

Overleaf: Taking the salute at the march-past which opened Hull's War Weapons Week (30 November-7 December 1940) was Lieutenant-General Sir Ronald Adam (GOC-in-C Northern Command). With the general were the Lord Mayor (Councillor Sydney Smith), the Sheriff (Mr R.G. Tarran), the Town Clerk (Mr A. Pickard) and the Under-Sheriff (Colonel Edgar Laverack). Other military gentlemen present included Vice-Admiral Holt, Captain the Viscount Hardinge and Commander Griffiths.

The Navy takes to the streets of Hull during War Weapons Week, The day's total of £736,112 being enough for two 'and a bit' destroyers. War Weapons Week was an appeal to save, not give money, by buying either National War Bonds, Defence Bonds, Saving Certificates or simply by putting cash into deposit accounts at the Post Office Savings Bank or the Hull Savings Bank.

SAVINGS BANK

HOURS OF BUSINESS

On and after the 4th October, 1940, the hours of business of this Bank will be:—

Monday to Thursday
10 a.m. to 4 p.m.

Saturday - 10 a.m. to 1 p.m.

Friday - 10 a.m. to 6 p.m.

The Friday evening opening is being suspended owing to the black-out, but any depositor who finds these amended hours inconvenient is asked to communicate with

THE ACTUARY,

GEORGE ST., HULL

when special arrangements will be made

Showing initiative with a table-top sale. *Harry Cartlidge Collection.*

Above: Workers queue
to contribute to Wings
for Victory at LNER
Wilmington. *Harry
Cartlidge Collection.*

*Right and opposite
page:* 383 Coast Defence
Battery, Royal Artillery,
help with the harvest
somewhere near Hull.
Imperial War Museum.

Farming

IN 1939, out of 29 million acres of arable land, 17 million was permanent grassland. Most farms were mixed farms of between 50 and 250 acres and although marketing boards existed and there was a guaranteed price for wheat, the industry was still depressed.

The coming of war was to change the face of British farming for ever. Under the supervision of the County War Agricultural Executive Committees, farmers were paid a subsidy of £2 per acre to plough up grassland; nearly two million acres being ploughed in 1940-41 alone. By the end of the war, nearly six million acres of permanent grassland had been ploughed for crops. Additional land was utilized for farming, thanks to Government financial assistance for drainage and land reclamation projects.

Farming became increasingly mechanized. At the start of the war, around 56,000 tractors were in use; by its end the total had risen to 203,000. Efficient use was made of combine harvesters, which were moved from farm to farm as they were needed; there were twice as many disc harrows in use by 1945 than there had been three years earlier; and a greater use was made of fertilizers.

Many dairy farmers installed milking machines; there were more cows than ever before, as well as an active campaign to get people to drink more milk.

One of the lesser-known functions of the County War Agricultural Executive Committees was to assess and classify farms according to productivity. If a farmer received a Classification he would at best be given assistance and equipment, but at the very worst he could be evicted. The most famous case of the latter involved a Hampshire farmer who was ordered out of his farm for failing to comply with a directive to plough four acres. The police were called in and things got out of hand, tragically so as it turned out. The farmer locked himself in his house and opened fire with a sporting gun wounding several policemen. The police resorted to tear gas but when that failed, armed officers were sent in and the farmer shot dead.

On a lighter note, depending on one's point of view, there is an interesting story of a farmer showing enterprise initiative. At the start of the war, fear of bombing and gas attacks resulted in many dog lovers having their pets destroyed. This particular farmer advertised that he could provide sanctuary for any number of dogs and would find them new homes; previous owners were welcome to telephone or write in at any time should they wish to find where their pet had gone. Enquirers were told that 'Rover has been found a home with some nice people at Beverley', or words to that effect. In fact, poor Rover was no longer with us, as his fur had been sold for use in fur-lined boots.

Land Army girls crew a home-made potato sowing machine. Reformed in June 1939, the Women's Land Army was 20,000 strong by September 1941 and apart from a uniform they were not really an army at all. They worked long hours, pay was poor, billeting often inadequate and leave virtually non-existent at just seven days a year. By June 1944, the strength of the WLA stood of 80,000, about 6,000 of which were in the Timber Corps, lumber-jacking often in remote parts of the country.

Royal Engineers normally assigned to taking care of an armoured train, look after the barley and wheat in September 1941. Helping with the harvest was typical of the work undertaken by UK-based army units, due to the fact that there was a shortage of manpower on the land and that, during 1940-41, about two million acres of permanent grassland had been ploughed for crops, followed in 1941-42 by another one and a half million acres.

Threshing machine at work, February 1941.

Dated 19 April 1941. Women aged 20 and 21 register for work under the recently-introduced Registration of Employment Order. By the end of the year, the scheme had been extended to include women up to the age of 30 and men up to the age of 46 and would eventually be extended even further to include all women aged between 18 and 51. Once registered, a person was invited along for an interview at the local Labour Exchange and, if not already in a job considered essential to the war effort, was asked to consider taking up work of national importance. Those refusing to do so could be compelled by the serving of a direction order to take a job.

Women trainees at a Government Training Centre, 12 February 1941. The centres had been established in the 1920s to teach new skills to unemployed males but from June 1940 the doors were thrown open to men over military age or those medically unfit for active service in an attempt to train sufficient additional workers for the expanding engineering and munitions industries. Courses were pretty basic and lasted for between one and two months, although students showing an aptitude were selected for further training. Towards the end of 1940, the decision was taken to admit women and over 100,000 would pass through GTCs between 1941 and the summer of 1943.

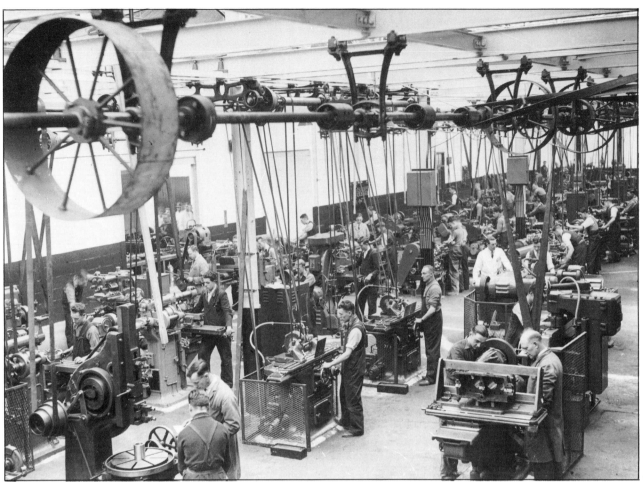

Just a few of an estimated 8,000 men attending Government Training Centres in December 1940. There were 14 centres at the start of the war, rising to a maximum of 38 before being reduced to 20 in 1943 as the number of trainees was declining.

Above and previous page (bottom): The outbreak of the war, 766,000 men were employed in the coal-mining industry, even though 61 per cent of coal was cut by machine. By the middle of 1941 there were only 690,000 and by May 1942 the figure had dropped to 524,000, due to younger men joining the armed forces or obtaining alternative employment. A plan to recall miners from the army was dropped in favour of an Essential Work Order being applied to the industry by Ernest Bevin. Until December 1943, young men were allowed to choose between the armed forces or working down the mines. Then lack of volunteers led to balloting whereby one in ten of those due for National Service were ordered down the mines, although fewer than three in ten would work at the coal-face. Around 21,000 Bevin Boys entered the mines. Many hated it, absenteeism was rife and it did little to address the fall in productivity. The pictures are of Bevin Boys going down Askern pit for the first time on 19 January 1944.

MINISTRY OF FUEL AND POWER.

COAL SUPPLIES DURING NOVEMBER & DECEMBER

The maximum quantity of coal (including briquettes and small anthracite) which may be supplied without licence to any controlled premises during the two months November-December, is twelve 10-stone or fifteen 1-cwt. bags.

If this quantity would raise your stock above 1½ tons you may obtain only sufficient to bring your stock to that total.

Coke, and anthracite of sizes exceeding 1¾, may be obtained without licence so long as your total stock of these two fuels is not raised above four tons.

It is an offence against the Defence Regulations to exceed these quantities without licence from the Local Fuel Overseer.

Consumers are asked to note that by mixing coke with coal a considerable reduction can be made in the consumption of coal.

Have you returned your Household Fuel Form (F.R.1) or your Fuel Assessment Form for Non-Industrial Establishments (F.R.2)? If not, it is essential, in your own interest, that this should be done without delay.

The Mines Department has announced that the information contained in these forms will later be used as a basis to determine the supplies allocated to your coal merchant, and failure to return these forms to the Local Fuel Overseer will probably result in fuel not being obtained during the difficult winter period when supplies are restricted.

With reference to the additional licences which are granted for stocking purposes by the Local Fuel Overseer, it should be noted that in the event of the introduction of a rationing scheme the amount of fuel which has been obtained through these licences will be deducted from any ration which may be fixed at a later date. Also, deliveries of fuel will not be allowed during the period January to March, excepting under the conditions specified in the licence.

H. LEGGOTT (Local Fuel Overseer, City and County of Kingston upon Hull).

H. W. MILLEN (Local Fuel Overseer, Haltemprice U.D.C.).

F. G. HILL (Local Fuel Overseer, Holderness R.D.C.).

NORMAN DIXON (Local Fuel Overseer, Withernsea U.D.C.)

From mid-1941, the provision of day-nursery places for the children of war workers was rapidly expanded and by the end of 1943 local authorities were able to provide places for 65,000 under-fives. This picture dates from November 1941, the one overleaf from July 1942.

Although heavily censored, these two pictures are believed to show part of the machine shops at the Blackburn Aircraft Company.

A Blackburn Skua on display in Hull alongside a captured Messerschmitt Bf109 fighter. The two-seater Skua was the Fleet Air Arm's first monoplane capable of operating from aircraft carriers and the first British-designed dive-bomber to enter squadron service.

The Fairey Barracuda II, powered by a Rolls-Royce Merlin 32 developing 1640hp, went into production at Brough towards the end of 1942, other manufacturers being Fairey at Stockport, and Boulton and Paul at Wolverhampton. Although the Barracuda had the handling qualities of a brick toilet, it compensated for the fact by its ability to carry a heavy pay-load of one 1610lb torpedo or up to 2,000lb in bombs.

The Blackburn Botha, a twin-engined torpedo bomber for Coastal Command, was in production when the war started. One of the first units to receive the plane was 608 (North Riding) Squadron Auxiliary Air force operating from Thornaby in a convoy escort role. Unfortunately, the Botha proved operationally unsuccessful and was withdrawn from front-line service being re-allocated to training units.

The Napier Sabre-powered Blackburn Firebrand first flew on 27 February 1942, deck-landing trials taking place a year later, the delay caused by modifications to the aerodynamics. What should have been one of the Fleet Air Arms' most formidable high-speed strike aircraft then underwent a series of major modifications with the result that the aircraft never saw combat. Only nine F1s and 12 TF2s were completed before the aircraft had to be virtually redesigned to take the Bristol Centaurus IX sleeve-valve engine; the first production model of this variant (TF111) flying in December 1943. The 27 aircraft in the production run were delivered to a trials unit in December 1944 and saw no operational use. Further variants were built after the war and Firebrand squadrons embarked on *HMS Eagle* and *HMS Illustrious* but were withdrawn from service during 1953.

If you've news of our munitions
KEEP IT DARK
Ships or planes or troop positions
KEEP IT DARK
Lives are lost through conversation
Here's a tip for the duration
When you've private information
KEEP IT DARK!

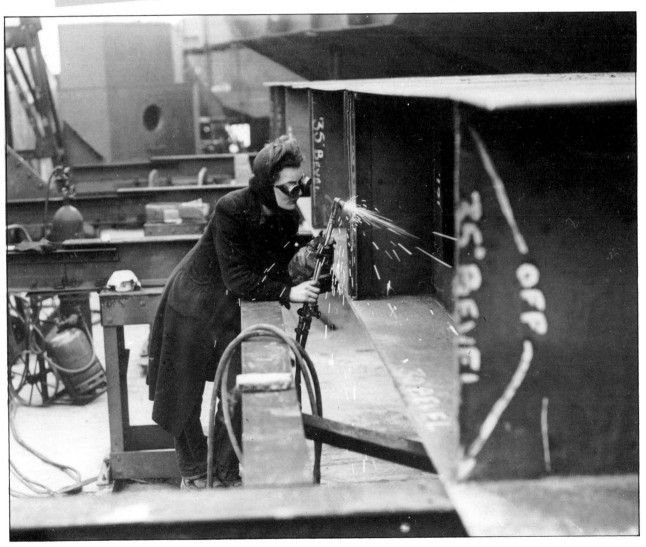

Lady welder at Richard Dunston (Hessle) Ltd. The yard was established by Henry Scarr in 1897 and taken over by Dunston in 1931, enabling Dunston's to build larger vessels than they would at their Thorne yard. The yard was known as Scarr's until the early 1960s. *Imperial War Museum.*

More scenes from Scarr's yard in 1944. *Top:* Some of the women workers. *Bottom:* Work proceeds on a Naval stores carrier.

Employees and their families gather for a launching ceremony.

Mrs Adamson and Mrs Atkinson perform the honours at a launching ceremony in April 1944. *Imperial War Museum.*

LcT1169 like LcT1315 should have been built by Sir William Arrol. Both craft were Type 4, of which around 800 were built between 1942 and 1945. They were designed to carry six 40-ton tanks or nine 30-ton tanks or twelve 3-ton trucks. As cargo carriers they could cope with 300 tonnes dead weight. Their Davey Paxman diesels gave them a speed of ten knots. *Imperial War Museum*

A Naval Auxiliary takes to the water in April 1944. The yard specialized in building vessels from prefabricated parts on four berths. Sixty per cent of the workforce were women. *Imperial War museum.*

LcT1315 at Scarrs. By using prefabricated sections, the yard was launching landing craft at the rate of one every seven days. This particular landing craft was scheduled to be built by Sir William Arrol of Alloa but appears to have been sub-contracted to Hessle. *Imperial War Museum*.

TID tugs in line ahead pass Hull on their journey from the builder's yard. *Harry Cartlidge Collection*.

The work goes on at Scarr's. Immediately following the launch of a vessel, work begins laying the next. Here a bottom plate is being lowered on to the ways. *Imperial War Museum.*

Air Raid Precautions

THE establishment of ARP arose out of Cabinet approval in 1935 for the spending of £100 pounds on planning for the contingency of war. It was widely believed that air-raids would be launched against our towns and cities within hours of the outbreak of war. By the end of 1938, nearly 1.4 million people had signed up for ARP duties, many in the wake of the Munich crisis and the growing realization that war was inevitable sooner rather than later.

Most ARPs were wardens whose job it was at the beginning of the war to enforce the black-out regulations and then later to judge the extent and type of any damage in their area so that the control centre could send the appropriate rescue services. Local knowledge was deemed to be vital for a warden to function effectively. They were expected to know where individual families sheltered during raids, where they were likely to go if the need for an alternative shelter arose.

The wardens were thus responsible for getting survivors out as speedily as possible and, once out, arranging for them to be taken to rest centres or to another shelter. More than 90 per cent of wardens were part-timers and around 20 per cent were women.

The lynch pin in the ARP network was the control centre of the two-wheeled variety with pumps powered by a four-cylinder petrol engine. There was also a four-wheeled heavy trailer pump built by both Sulzer and Tangye and these were powered with Ford V8 engines. The AFS were also supplied with self-contained fire engines, the basic model being based upon either a Fordson or Leyland chassis and armed with a 900gpm Sulzer pump. The other type, known as an extra-heavy unit, was again based on a Fordson or Leyland chassis but equipped with a pump capable of delivering 1400gpm through six branches. All AFS units were painted battleship grey and lacked the brass and chrome adornments of regular machines.

On 30 August 1939, all AFS and regular units were issued with steel helmets and respirators and the Home Office announced that the weekly rates of pay for full-time AFS crews would be £3 for men, £2 for women, £1 25s for youths aged 17 to 18, and £1 for youths aged 16 to 17.

As the bombing continued into 1941, the groundswell of opinion in the fire service favouring a nationalized force grew. The attitude of local authorities to the fire service was amazingly varied, ranging from excellent to totally apathetic. In some towns the local authorities had failed to decide where all rescue and emergency aid was to be co-ordinated.

Under the direct orders of the control centres were the first-aid parties and the rescue men. The rescue men had the really back-breaking tasks as they searched through debris for survivors, often amidst fire and with the ever-present danger of explosion from fractured gas mains.

The ARP organization embraced many other bodies ranging from the Women's Voluntary Service (WVS) — who in the early stages looked after the 'bombed out' as well as crewing canteens and rest centres — to the police and fire services.

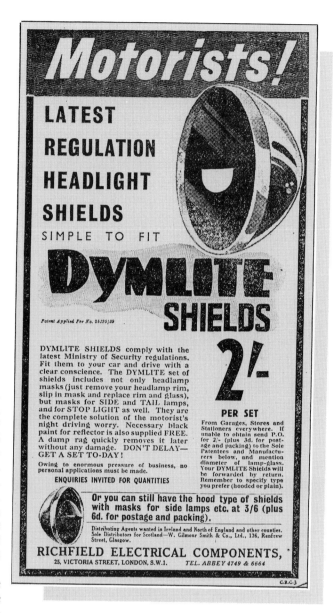

In the 1930s, Hull already possessed a highly professional fire brigade, but despite its high standard of training and up-to-date equipment, it could not be expected to cope with all the emergencies arising out of a major air-raid. So along with other towns and cities, Hull set about forming an Auxiliary Fire Service (AFS).

AFS equipment usually consisted of trailer pumps designed for towing behind any suitable vehicle. These trailer pumps of which there were four types, had a pumping capacity of between 120gpm and 900gpm and were manufactured by a number of companies including Coventry-Climax, Dennis, Scammell, and Worthington-Simpson. All of these types were provided with towing vehicles for each trailer pump and it was not uncommon to see fire crews having to man-handle pumps to blitz fires.

On the evening of 18 April 1941, Home Secretary Herbert Morrison met with Sir George Gater (secretary to the Minister of Home Security), Sir Arthur Dixon (head of the fire service division of the Home Office) and Commander Firebrace (of the London Fire Brigade). Within four hours the principles of a National Fire Service (NFS) had been thrashed out and on 22 May, the Bill received the Royal Assent.

The broad plan was to amalgamate the UK's existing 1,400 brigades into 12 regions, each being further sub-divided into fire forces. The Government was to undertake the whole cost of the emergency element of the service and to pay 25 per cent towards the normal annual running costs of the regular brigade.

The most important ARP work was preventative as in evacuation and the use of shelters. Shelters were marketed to the population of Hull during the spring of 1939 and could be purchased locally or even by mail-order. The Hudson indoor shelter, it was announced, was made from 'Dalzo rust-resisting plates and weighing about 13cwt . . .the design has been submitted to the Home Office who state that it is suitable for four persons and that it will give admirable protection against splinter and blast of high-explosive bombs and overhead cover from incendiary bombs when properly sandbagged'.

This particular model was advertised at just £30, 'supplied in one piece' and thus requiring 'no assembly in situ'. A report on the Hudson stated: "For houses in which it is not convenient to construct a room to afford the necessary protection without involving expensive structural alterations the shelter appears well suited to providing a good refuge for an average suburban family."

Gas mask drill in the Council Chamber, Thursday, 27 February 1941.

The ARP anti-gas training school classroom, photographed by Harry Cartlidge.

"Can you see me mother?" Trainees at the anti-gas school. The van in the background was a mobile testing unit for gas masks. Vehicles of this type would visit factories and the city centre so that people could walk in and have their gas masks checked for leaks. *Harry Cartlidge Collection*

The anti-gas school.

Members of Boulevard Civil Defence depot c1943-44. *Central Library Collection.*

Wellington Lane depot personnel, 27 February 1944. *Central Library Collection.*

Men and vehicles on parade at Wellington Lane depot in September 1944. *Central Library Collection.*

A first-aid party on exercise c1941. Each party consisted of four men and a driver, all experienced first-aiders having been trained by the Red Cross or St John's Ambulance Brigade. Their main task was to help the rescue men release trapped casualties and then administer what aid they could before deciding whether or not a casualty needed further treatment at a first-aid post (FAP) or hospital. There was usually one post to every 15,000 people but cities the size of Hull were also equipped with mobile units capable of reinforcing a hard-pressed fixed post or even a hospital. *Collection C.J.Hardy*

Rescue men and first-aid party bring a casualty out of the rubble. This picture is not of an exercise, it is a real event.

Black-Out Tomorrow: 4.35 p.m.

SUMMER-TIME ends at 3 a.m. tomorrow, and from next week the black-out will descend on Britain an hour earlier. The clock goes BACK.

Many offices and warehouses are planning to close earlier, but, even so, workers will have to go home in the black-out.

The departure of B.S.T. is regretted by shopkeepers and business men, but farmers and others who have to start work early in the day welcome the return of G.M.T. Shopkeepers deplore the change (see Page Nine).

Make note of the revised black-out times :
Tonight   5.36*—6.55a.m.†
Tomorrow 4.35†—6.57 a.m.†

* Summer Time
† Winter Time

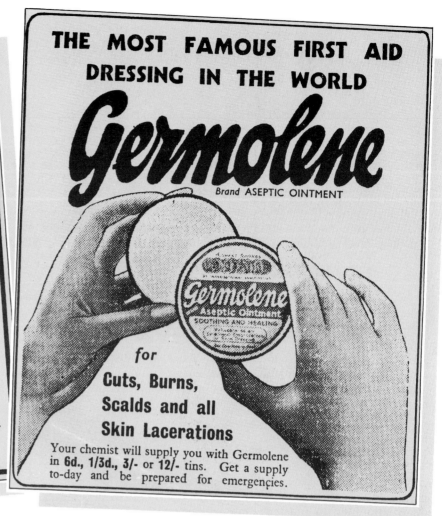

British Red Cross Society dance at Wenlock Barracks, 23 May 1941.

This photograph of a fire amidst three stacks of corn sheaves, dated 4 September 1940, was passed by the censor for publication. The theory was that the fire had been started by incendiary bombs dropped from an enemy aircraft. AFS men and farm workers deal with the smouldering stacks.

Dated 2 September 1940, this might be the same fire as on the previous page yet this particular photograph carried a 'Not to be published' stamp from the Press and Censorship Bureau.

NFS fire crew tackle a blaze in a small factory hit by incendiaries.

Leyland/Metz turntable ladder delivered to Hull in 1936 was the largest of its type in the country with a 167ft extending ladder. Once war had been declared the acquisition of German fire-fighting equipment (Metz being a German company) was naturally out of the question, so the gap was filled by Merryweather and Sons. *Leyland Trucks.*

HRH The Princess Royal meets members of Hull's AFS during her visit to the city on 8 April 1941.

Their Majesties King George VI and Queen Elizabeth chat to ARP personnel during their visit to Hull on 6 August 1941.

Winston Churchill paid a visit to Hull during his whistle-stop tour of Sheffield and the North-East. Here he inspects ARP messenger boys. It was these young men upon whom the Control Centre had to rely when the telephone links were cut.

Railway workers fill sandbags at one of the local LNER sidings. *Harry Cartlidge Collection.*

The Home Guard

SOME of the activities of *Dad's Army* can now be relied upon to bring a wry smile, but its establishment arose out of a very real fear. When the Germans invaded Holland and Belgium in May 1940, their paratroops played a leading role and Britain also feared that airborne soldiers might be used against her to establish a bridgehead prior to a seaborne assault.

On 14 May, Anthony Eden went on radio and appealed for men aged 17 to 65 to form anti-paratroop units guarding installations like factories, ports, power stations and railways. There was a tremendous response. At first, units were mainly groups of employees protecting their own works premises and initially they were called Local Defence Volunteers (LDV), although more than one wit re-christened them "Look, Duck and Vanish". The name was changed to Home Guard in July 1940.

The pre-arranged signal for a paratroop landing was to be the ringing of Church Bells on receipt of the codeword *Cromwell*. On 7 September 1940, the codeword was issued by HQ Home Command, not because an invasion had taken place but because it was deemed that one was likely at this time. On learning that *Cromwell* had been issued, some local commanders commandered churches and ordered the bells rung. The Home Guard was stood to, ready to do its stuff even if weapons and ammunition were still in short supply. *Cromwell* remained in force for 12 days and when lifted the country was rife with rumours that a seaborne invasion had been beaten off by setting the sea ablaze with flaming oil; barbecuing the Germans and their assault craft.

From August 1940, Home Guard units were affiliated to local county regiments and regular NCOs helped with weapons training. In February 1941, ranks the same as in the army had been introduced and all officers reviewed as to their abilities, and equipment improved with supplies of automatic weapons and anti-tank rifles.

By the summer of 1943, the strength of the Home Guard stood at 1.75 million men in 1,100 battalions and was being increasingly used to give 16 and 17-year-olds a taste of the army before call up. Gone were the broom shanks, assorted cutlery from long-forgotten

A Home Guardsman keeps his eye on things following the discovery of a bomb crater in a nearby field after an air-raid. The picture carries no date but, judging from the equipment carried by the guardsman, it must have been taken after August 1940 because he appears to be wearing a county unit patch just below his left shoulder tab. *C.J.Hardy Collection.*

colonial wars and 12-bore shotguns. In their place came increasingly sophisticated weapons and once the danger of invasion had subsided, guardsmen took over anti-aircraft and coast defence batteries from regular troops.

From the spring of 1944, the Home Guard took over routine and security duties from regular units as well as continuing to take part in exercises with British and Allied troops.

One of the two endearing qualities of the Home Guard was that it stood the social and class structure of the UK on its head. The War Office insisted that commissions and promotions within the Home Guard had to be on merit and not on class or education. This meant that a factory manager could find himself being ordered about by one of the work labourers because the labourer just happened to be an ex-regular soldier. It was also possible that your train ticket might be inspected or your bus ticket clipped by a fully-commissioned Home Guard captain or major.

The second endearing quality was that protrayed by Captain Mainwaring and his lads in the television series. Every unit has its stories to tell. My own father managed to mistake a prize bull for a paratrooper and shot it dead with the only bullet he'd been issued with. Then there was the local platoon due to be inspected by a 'brass hat' from Catterick. The men with boots and brasses polished, battledress smartly creased, rifles cleaned and bayonets sparkling, stood and waited for the staff car to arrive. And waited and waited and waited. That is until the local pub opened, whereupon an orderly retreat to the bar took place. While they were sipping their pints, they saw through the window a staff car, pass along the street, its occupants vainly searching for the parade.

On another occasion a unit decided to test-fire its newly acquired Blacker Bombard mortar. The weapon was set up and aimed towards some woods which a scouting party was supposed to have cleared in advance. The mortar bomb did not contain an explosive charge, so after it had been fired the idea was to go and retrieve it. The bomb landed near the middle of the wood and out of the trees shot a perplexed and somewhat flustered pair of young lovers.

Hull Home Guardsmen take part in a street-fighting exercise. *Imperial War Museum.*

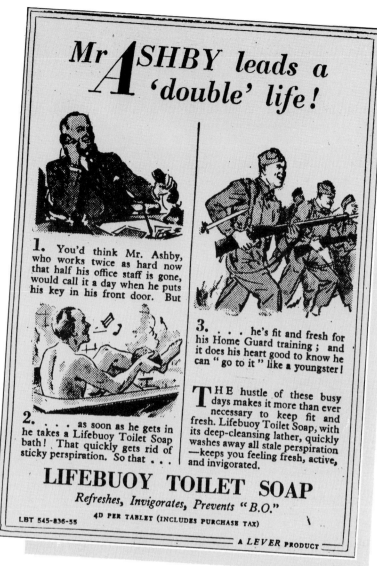

The Home Guard, aided and abetted by the local Constabulary, come together in an arresting combination to apprehend a group of 'invaders' during an exercise held in Hull on 20 July 1941.

Policemen tackle the enemy during Exercise Ajax. *Lieutenant O'Brien.*

The Police with some of their captives. *Lieutenant O'Brien.*

Invasion Scare

ON 22 June 1941, the Germans committed one of their more fatal blunders of the war when they attacked the Soviet Union on a 1,800 mile front with three million troops, 3,580 tanks, 1,860 combat aircraft and 600,000 vehicles. According to Hitler and the military planners, this particular *blitzkrieg* would last a few months at most. On 2 September, invading troops clashed with Soviet forces defending Moscow and on 1 December, Panzer troops could see the winter sunlight reflecting off the domes of the Kremlin only nine miles away.

The immediate threat of a German invasion of the United Kingdom had subsided towards the end of 1940 with the Luftwaffe unable to gain air superiority over the Royal Air Force and the Kriegsmarine's logistical nightmare of finding sufficient invasion craft and surface warships with which to attempt the crossing of the English Channel. However, the possible defeat of the Soviet Union renewed speculation that the Germans might attempt a surprise landing, possibly with paratroops, and schemes were drawn up for the evacuation of schools and colleges away from the fighting should such an event arise.

In Hull, the planning and co-ordinating fell upon the shoulders of Mr R.C.Moore, the Director of Education, and his staff. In the event of it becoming necessary to evacuate Hull's children, Mr Moore and his staff would establish their headquarters at the College of Arts and Crafts but if this building was damaged and unfit for use, then they would transfer to Clifton Street School. Two other schools, Westbourne Street and St George's Road, were earmarked as the third and fourth reserve headquarters respectively.

The plan devised comprised of two phases, first warning and second warning.

On receipt of the first warning, it was the responsibility of the Director of Education to see that the headteacher or teacher in charge of each school was notified of the same. Any teacher away from Hull learning that the first warning had been issued, was

Up a tree with 37 Searchlight Regiment manning an observation post at Cottingham. *Imperial War Museum*

expected to return at once without waiting to be officially recalled and if the warning was received immediately prior to a school holiday, then the holiday was cancelled, the school to remain open for both staff and pupils. If the warning was received during a school holiday, then the school was to reopen as soon as possible.

After receipt of the first warning, all out-of-school activities — swimming, handicraft and domestic subjects — were to be cancelled, the handicraft and domestic subject centres were to close and their staff had to report to their nearest elementary school.

The second warning, to be issued by the authorities when invasion was imminent, would result in schools going to a complete state of readiness for evacuation. Arrangements were made so that key teachers living in Hull would be notified as soon as possible, day or night, that the second warning had been received. These key teachers were then responsible for contacting a second group of teachers in the same district and so on, until all teachers whose addresses were in the city had been notified.

Various arrangements existed for getting schools opened depending on when the warning was received, but a rota system was also to come into force so that two teachers would be on duty at certain schools at any time of the day or night, seven days a week, so that messages and instructions could be delivered. These schools were designated 'focal' schools and were to act as the contact point for several other schools. For example, Villa Place Girls acted as the focal school for Villa Place Junior and Infants, T.B.Holmes Boys, West Dock Avenue Senior Boys, West Dock Avenue Junior Boys and West Dock Avenue Infants as well as Scarborough Street Juniors and Infants, Springburn Street Boys and St Wilfred's Roman Catholic School.

The Technical College was the focal school for Wawne Street (Boys, Girls and Infants), Thomas Stratten (Boys, Girls and Infants), T.B.Holmes Girls and Infants and the Hebrew School.

The local authorities were also required to draw up a list of all schools or centres in their areas where there were facilities for preparing meals. Category 'C' buildings were those with cooking facilities to prepare 50 meals at a time. Category 'E' had equipment for only 30 at a time, whilst Category 'F' could provide 200 meals and were stocked accordingly.

An official announcement said: "The conditions which may obtain in the event of invasion cannot be accurately forecast, but the Board do not doubt that they can rely on all concerned to comply readily with any instructions that may emanate from competent authorities and to use their own initiative in dealing with unforseen contingencies."

However, not every school was to be evacuated. Some had been told to 'stay put and carry on', whatever that was supposed to mean in the middle of a possible full-blown enemy attack. This was not a policy decided upon by Hull. It was Government policy in that: "Different considerations arise in the case of residential schools. The Government's view is that such schools, in common with other classes of the population, should conform to the policy of 'Stay put and carry on', ie they should keep their pupils unless they receive instructions to the contrary from the competent authorities."

The schools not scheduled for evacuation under this policy were: Cottage Pasture Camp School at Etton, the Children's Homes in Hessle High Road, Park Avenue Special School at Barrow Hall, Nursery Hostel, Wressle House, the Municipal Training College in Halifax, The Remand House in Hull, the Castle Howard School, The Park Avenue Special School at Ripley, Derbyshire, and the Malton Street Special School at Foxholes near Malton.

The local independent schools were encouraged to maintain contacts with the Local Education

Authority, so that they too could take the appropriate action on receipt of the first and second warnings. In Hull, these schools were the Grammar School, Hymers College, Marist College and St Mary's Roman Catholic Secondary School.

HRH the Princess Royal inspects troops deployed on anti-invasion duties.

If the invader came, the job of the Home Guard was to attempt to contain the enemy until the arrival of regular troops. But in September 1940, when this picture was taken, about half of the 27 divisions in Home Forces were virtually untrained and most were under-equipped.

The balloon barrage was under the jurisdiction of 33 Group Royal Air Force, with its HQ at Newcastle upon Tyne, although this was later transferred to Hull and then to Park Head, Sheffield. This Harry Cartlidge photograph shows a barrage balloon being lowered at Hull.

A small crowd gathers to watch a balloon being lowered. *Harry Cartlidge Collection.*

A barrage balloon being raised at Hull Docks. *Harry Cartlidge Collection.*

The Hull balloon barrage comprised 942 and 943 Squadrons.

Barrage balloon takes to the water aboard the *Norman Wade*.

Cook Bill Downs works out his latest culinary masterpiece.

"For what we are about to receive". Meal time aboard the *Norman Wade*.

The accounts officer, back at Hull from paying the crew of the *Norman Wade*.

The accounts officer and crew of the *Norman Wade*.

The view from Harry Cartlidge's dock office window. In the distance the balloon barge *Norman Wade* is on station.
Harry Cartlidge Collection.

Thompson Haslar mobile smoke screen generator on test. Some 900 were built by the Wolverhampton-based John Thompson Organization and were deployed around all major towns and cities. Some of the units eventually finished up in North Africa.

Action Stations! Anti-aircraft battery personnel race to their positions during an exercise for the benefit of the Press.

Northern Command anti-aircraft battery range-finder and predictor crews closed-up ready for action. This picture is thought to be of the battery at Hedon.

One of the
heavy anti-
aircraft guns
d e f e n d i n g
Hull (possibly
at Hedon) The
crew are 'put-
ting one up the
spout'.

Searchlights
probe the night
sky in April
1940.

One of Hull's searchlights, 5 March 1940.

From 1942, the Home Guard took over the manning of a large number of AA gun-sites and two-rocket batteries. The rockets were solid-fuelled and could be fired in salvoes of about 100 at a time. Accelerating to over 1,000mph in a second and a half, the rockets made a tremendous noise. Because anti-aircraft and two-batteries had to be manned mainly at night, shift workers were usually ruled out. Also a man had to be physically fit to work on a rocket site. A training site where live firings took place, was built near Cleethorpes.

The Bombing

IT had always been thought that once war was declared, our towns and cities would be subjected to massive air-raids by the Luftwaffe: hence the elaborate and relatively efficient evacuation of children, expectant mothers and the disabled from likely target areas; hence the reasoning behind the black-out regulations; the establishment of civil defence and rescue units and the siting of some barrage balloon squadrons and anti-aircraft batteries.

That the raids never started is one of the factors as to why the period up to the German invasion of Norway is now known as the 'phoney war'. The perceived inactivity of the Luftwaffe led to thousands of evacuees returning home, full-time air-raid precautions staff being made redundant, auxiliary fire-service crews being branded as shirkers who had simply joined the AFS to get out of being conscripted into the army.

But the Luftwaffe was in fact very active during this period, its operations restricted to military objectives, mine-laying, strikes against our shipping, reconnaissance flights and clashing with the RAF and the French Air Force.

Our first casualties were self-inflicted. On the morning of 6 September 1939, Hurricanes of 56 Squadron clashed with Spitfires of 74 Squadron in the skies above Suffolk, Pilot Officer Montague Hutton-Harrop of 74 Squadron becoming the first RAF pilot to be killed in combat.

His colleague, Pilot Officer Frank Rose, became the first pilot to survive a forced landing, shaken but otherwise unhurt, after he managed to bring his shot-up Hurricane down to earth at Whersted, between Ipswich and Manningtree.

Further south, aircraft of 65 Squadron were fired on by a number of anti-aircraft batteries because the gunners could not read morse, thus failing to recognise the significance of the message the pilots were flashing on their aircraft downward indentification lights.

The first bomb to fall on England occured at just before 8.00am on Sunday, 24 September 1939, when a house at Headington, near Oxford, suffered a direct hit from a practice bomb accidentally dropped by an RAF aircraft. The bomb failed to detonate but even so, a young evacuee was seriously injured.

Two days later saw the loss of the Luftwaffe's first aircraft in combat against British forces, when a Dornier 18D was shot down by Skuas of 803 Squadron operating from HMS *Ark Royal*.

The first attack by the Luftwaffe upon the British mainland was carried out on Monday, 16 October 1939 by nine Junkers JU88s of 1/K930 against warships in the Firth of Forth. Damage was caused to the cruisers HMS *Southampton,* HMS *Edinburgh* and the destoryer HMS *Mohawk*. Two of the aircraft were shot down by Spitfires of 602 Squadron, whilst another was damaged but returned safely to base.

In Hull, the air-raid sirens had sounded the first ominous warning of the war on Monday, 4 September. It was a false alarm but it was the first of over 800 alerts that the city would endure of which no less than 82 would result in bombs and incendiaries being dropped.

WHEN THE SIRENS GO

A notice broadcast yesterday by the Lord Privy Seal's Office said:—

IN the event of threatened air raids, warnings will be given in urban areas by sirens or hooters, which will be sounded in some places by short intermittent blasts and in other places by a warbling note changing every few seconds.

The warning may also be given by short blasts on police whistles. No hooter or siren may be sounded except on the instructions of the police.

When you hear any of these sounds— TAKE SHELTER.

And do not leave your shelter until you hear the " Raiders Passed " signal, which will be given by continuously sounding the sirens or hooters for two minutes on the same note.

Although Hull itself would be spared bombs for some months, the Luftwaffe were very active, launching strikes against merchant ships and fishing vessels in the North Sea, mining the approaches to the Humber and undertaking a number of photo-reconnaissance missions over the area in general.

On Saturday, 21 October, the towns and cities of Grimsby, Hull, Doncaster, York and Lincoln all received 'condition yellow' air alerts at 2.15pm as a group of Heinkel He 115Bs approached the Humber. Grimsby and Hull went to 'condition red' and Hurricanes of 46 Squadron were scrambled to intercept the intruders. Three of the enemy aircraft were shot down, two crashing in the Wash, the other going down five miles east of Spurn Head.

One merchant ship, the *Capitaine Edmond Laborie* was sunk her survivors being landed at Grimsby. The Luftwaffe's attacks against shipping and the mining of the Humber continued into 1940, the first local casualty being the requisitioned trawler *Benvolio* mined in the approaches on 23 February 1940.

On the night of 18-19 June, coastal districts from Teesside in the north-east to Portsmouth in the south-west were placed on the alert. Bombs fell on a number of places including Barton-on-Humber, Alnwick, Canvey Island, Cambridge and Southend, leaving a total of ten civilians killed and 26 injured. For the next week or so, the east coast was subjected to nightly incursions, the attacking planes splitting off into small flights to raid from the Tees to Bristol but inflicting little damage and few casualties.

Just what was the purpose behind these tactics remains a mystery. The Luftwaffe passed up the chance to inflict damage on a number of wide open targets; they seemed to be concerned more with putting our defences to the test. One theory put forward is that these raids were being carried out to gauge timings in order to give ground attack support to an airborne invasion. It would certainly go some way to explaining why the Luftwaffe appeared pre-occupied with dropping bombs in open country rather than on military or industrial targets.

On the afternoon of 1 July, a Heinkel He111-4 of 3/KG4 attacked the oil storage facility at Saltend, setting one of the tanks on fire. However, Oberleutnant Koch's victory celebrations would be short-lived. Turning for home he was intercepted and shot down by Yellow Section, 616 Squadron. The Oberleutnant and his crew took to their dingy and were picked up by the sloop HMS *Black Swan*.

In August, the bombing reached a new intensity

following both the rejection of Hitler's peace proposals and the Luftwaffe's intention to smash the RAF as a prelude to invasion. Although the bulk of operations were directed against the RAF, Portsmouth was attacked by 500 aircraft on the 24th resulting in 117 people killed and 99 seriously injured. The night of the 24th-25th saw raids against Tyneside, Wearside, the Tees, York, Ripon, Driffield, and Hull, where six people were killed and ten seriously injured. Three nights later, the porter's lodge and maternity home on Hedon Road took a direct hit but, thankfully, there were no serious casualties. For the rest of the year, attacks on Hull would remain light, although there would be alerts almost daily.

But by October 1940 things were not going entirely in the Luftwaffe's favour. The blitz on London had developed into a war of attrition proving costly in aircrews and machines; operational bomber strength

Luftwaffe target information relating to the Alexandra and the King George Docks in Hull. This photograph probably dates from before the war but was updated on 12 September 1940. The targets identified are A Alexandra Dock (Luftwaffe reference 4225); 1 the sea lock; 2 the pier, and 3 the dry docks. Target D is the Alexandra Dock cold-storage plant (Luftwaffe reference 5625). Target B is the King George Dock and within this are the subsidiary targets 4 the sea lock; 5 the pumphouse; 6 dock warehouses; 7 warehouses; 8 dry docks; and C the silo, which again had its own specific target reference of 5621. *Central Library Collection.*

had been whittled from over 1,300 aircraft to around 700 and, although new aircraft were reaching squadrons, there was a desperate shortage of spares. By the beginning of November, Göring was forced to call off daylight attacks and although London was to remain the primary target, emphasis was to be placed upon the destruction of ports and armaments centres.

It was shortly after 7.00pm that the sirens warned the citizens of Coventry of impending attack and when the all-clear was given 11 hours later, one-third of the city centre had been completely destroyed under a rain of 1,200 high-explosive bombs, 50 parachute mines and 30,000 incendiaries. In Germany, a new word was coined meaning the destruction of a city from the air — 'Coventrated'.

Before the end of the month, Liverpool, Southampton, and Birmingham had been subjected to heavy raids. In December, weather conditions were such that for 15 nights the Luftwaffe were unable to get into the air. However, there were 11 major and five moderately heavy raids, with London suffering three major and 12 light attacks and Birmingham, Portsmouth, Liverpool and Leicester were blitzed. In Sheffield, 760 people were killed as the result of two heavy raids.

GB 56 37 b

Hull

Genst. 5. Abt. November 1941

Nur für den Dienstgebrauch

19 Ölmühlen und Speisefettfabriken

Bild Nr. 427 L 60

Länge (westl. Greenw.): 0° 20′ 20″ Breite: 53° 45′ 05″ Bildmitte

Karte 1 : 100 000
GB/E 10

Aufnahme vom 3. 9. 39

Mißweisung: — 10° 49′ (Mitte 1941) Zielhöhe über NN 5 m

Maßstab etwa 1 : 16 000

500   0   500   1000 m

Reconnaissance photograph of Hull taken on the 3 September 1939 and issued to Luftwaffe units in November 1941. No targets have been highlighted by the Luftwaffe planners but it is thought that the photograph was taken to pinpoint the oil and fat mills. *Central Library Collection.*

February 1941 brought eight light attacks on Hull, killing a total of 21 people and seriously injuring 39 others. The following month the Luftwaffe launched heavy raids against Portsmouth, Merseyside, Plymouth, Clydeside, Bristol and Hull, the latter being attacked heavily during the early hours of the 19th by no less than 187 bombers of Luftflotte 3. On the night of Tuesday 18 March, the Luftwaffe's primary target was to be Hull with secondary raids against Southampton and London.

In all, 464 long-range and 19 light bombers were assigned to operations, the attack on Hull opening at 8.40pm. By the time the last 12 aircraft of 1/KG27 had flown over the city at a little before 4.00am the following morning, no less than 378 German air crews had claimed to have found their primary target dropping a grand total of 316 tonnes of high-explosive bombs and 77,016 incendiaries.

But with visibility becoming poorer as the night progressed, some of the attackers were wide of the mark, their bombs and incendiaries falling on Scarborough, Beverley and Driffield. Even so, the damage inflicted upon Hull was severe, resulting in 91 people killed and 70 seriously injured. Despite the Humber anti-aircraft batteries firing 2,500 rounds and 56 aircraft being scrambled on offensive fighter sweeps, no enemy aircraft were shot down.

On the night of 31 March, the raiders struck Hull again, when 47 bombers dropped 39 tonnes of high-explosives, 32 parachute mines and 22,688 incendiaries. The dock installations were the target but again cloud, poor visibility and rain squalls led to bombs falling over a wide area. The Infirmary was badly damaged, but the ARP Control Centre at the corner of Ferensway and Spring Bank took a direct hit from a mine and among the casualties was Hull's Deputy Medical Officer of Health, Dr David Diamond. About 500 houses were damaged and 52 people were killed.

In April there were eight minor raids, although the night of the 15th saw Hull's worst incident of the war when a parachute mine scored a direct hit on a public shelter in Ellis Terrace, Holderness Road, killing 60.

On the 5 May, Hull and Plymouth were assigned to inexperienced crews as the Luftwaffe classed both as easy to find, whilst experienced air crews were assigned to raid Glasgow, Clydeside, Merseyside and Newcastle upon Tyne. In all 12 aircraft attacked Hull, dropping 14 tonnes of high-explosives, causing some damage in the docks, but most of the bombs fell harmlessly in rural areas.

Two nights later, Hull was subjected to a major attack along with Liverpool and Birkenhead. A total

Target GB5625b, the Külhaüser (cold-storage warehouses) at Alexandra Dock. This particular picture appears to come from an *objekbilder*, a booklet of photographs issued to air crew as an aid to identifying targets. The quality pictures used often left much to be desired. For a start they were not necessarily taken from the air. The majority were reworked postcards with backgrounds masked, targets highlighted and additional information overprinted. They could also be years out of date. The sources of the pictures ranged from private snapshots to up-to-date reconnaissance pictures. The Germans had no problem in getting hold of British postcards as many were printed in Bavaria. *Central Library Collection.*

of 346 bombers and 18 night fighters were assigned to operations, 72 bombers attacking Hull with 110 tonnes of high explosives and 9,648 incendiaries. From the Luftwaffe's point of view, the attack on Hull achieved excellent results. At least 30 major and over 100 smaller fires were started and damage to both residential and commercial property was extensive as the bulk of the bombs fell on the city centre.

Around 32,000 homes were destroyed or damaged and upwards of 10,000 people made homeless.

The following night the raiders returned. However, Hull was not the intended target; the Luftwaffe planned a major attack against Sheffield but unfavourable weather conditions led to aircraft being redirected en route. The result was that 120 aircraft arrived over Hull where the clear skies allowed them to bomb visually, dropping 167 tonnes of high-explosives and 19,467 incendiaries.

The damage caused was again extensive, compounding the destruction of the previous attack. By now extensive damage had been inflicted on Alexandra Dock, Riverside Quay, Albert Dock and William Wright Dock. Only two of the city's big flour mills remained, Spillers, Gilboys, Rishworth, Ingleby and Lofthouse had been completely destroyed. Paragon Station was out of action and the city's gas supply cut. Casualties for the two nights were 450 killed, 350 seriously injured and several hundred slightly injured.

Hull's 50th air-raid occured on the night of 2 June, but by now the intensity of Luftwaffe operations in the west was in decline as units were transferred east for the coming invasion of Russia.

On the night of 17-18 July, Hull suffered a heavy raid when Luftflotte 3 attacked with 108 aircraft dropping 173.9 tonnes of high-explosives and 6,194 incendiaries, causing considerable damage and killing 140 people. From now on, raids were sporadic although alerts still constant. On the night of 23 June 1943, 25 people were killed when Hull was raided by 33 aircraft, whilst 26 people were killed in a raid on the night of 25 July, although one of the attackers was shot down by anti-aircraft gunfire and two by Flying Officer Cowles of 604 Squadron.

The last raid occured on the night of 17-18 March 1945, when a force of 18 aircraft were sortied. Eleven of these aircraft crossed the east coast between Scarborough and Walton-on-the-Naze and an attack was mounted against Hull, resulting in 12 people being killed and 22 seriously injured.

In all the city had suffered 824 alerts and 82 raids, resulting in 1,258 civilians killed. On the city's housing stock, 4,415 were destroyed and 152,000 damaged (some more than once).

Paid members of the Observer Corps worked a 48-hour week, unpaid members helped out in the evenings and at weekends. The Corps was divided into five areas which were then sub-divided into Groups. Hull was part of 10 Group with the HQ at York.

The porter's lodge at the maternity home, Hedon Road was hit by a bomb on the night of 27/28 August 1940. Fortunately there were no casualties. *Central Library Collection.*

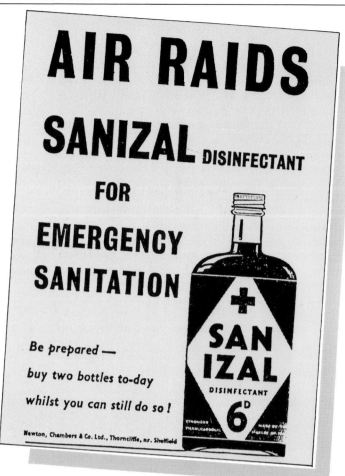

Parachute mine down at the East Hull Estate. *Central Library Collection*

Damage to houses in Kirby Street following a raid on 26 February 1940 in which one person was killed. *Central Library Collection.*

Damage inflicted on the East Hull Estate in February 1941. During that month, Hull was raided on eight occasions resulting in 21 people killed and 39 seriously injured. *Central Library Collection.*

Fountain Road, February 1941. *Central Library Collection*

Troops and workmen clear debris in Prospect Street. *Central Library Collection.*

Damping down the still smouldering ruins in Prospect Street. *Central Library Collection.*

Crash Evacuation

ON the night of 14 November 1940 the city of Coventry was devastated in an air-raid lasting 11 hours and although this was bad enough for anyone caught underneath the falling bombs and incendiaries, things could have been much worse. For instance, if all the attacking aircraft had passed over the target area within the space of half an hour or so, instead of arriving at intervals throughout the night, the concentrated effect of thousands of incendiaries and hundreds of high-explosive bombs might well have created the conditions necessary for a fire storm.

As it was the fires quickly spread, especially in the city centre, the heart of which was medieval in character with many timber-framed buildings huddled round the Cathedral in narrow winding streets, back alleys and courtyards.

From the air, Coventry's suffering could be seen by German aircrews as they were flying over the English Channel. Some mistook the faint red glow for a beacon of some sort, possibly for night fighters, and it was only as they got nearer that they realized that it was Coventry on fire. On the ground the glow from the burning city could be seen as far away as Derby, Nottingham, Birmingham and Rugby.

In Coventry itself chaos reigned. The Civil Defence Control Centre had taken a direct hit and local communications were virtually non-existent, relying on the undoubted bravery of young teenagers and Boy Scouts who made their way through what must have seemed like Dantes Inferno, relaying messages to police, fire crews, first-aid parties and rescue squads alike. To add to Coventry's problems, all roads in and out of the city were blocked with debris, the railway line severely damaged and the railway station all but destroyed. Help was on its way from a number of nearby towns as well as a convoy of fire-fighting vehicles from the London Fire Brigade but it would be hours before any relief got through. The Civil authorities were close to losing control.

But why mention Coventry in a book about Hull? Because one of the lessons learned was the need for a crash evacuation scheme — in other words, a system whereby those made homeless by a blitz-type raid could be evacuated quickly and effectively instead of being left to their own devices.

Once again, the task of organizing the scheme fell to Mr R.C.Moore, Director of Education.

By January 1941, Mr Moore and his staff had worked out a scheme to replace a preliminary plan hurriedly devised in the weeks following the attack on Coventry. The headquarters from which the evacuation would be controlled were to be at Blenkin Street School, Witham, but if this building was damaged or destroyed, then Endike Lane School would be used. In the event of both of these buildings being unusable the headquarters would be housed at Bricknell Avenue School.

The city was divided into ten divisions, each with a divisional headquarters and each divisional headquarters having three reserve headquarters. For example, Division One's headquarters were at Wheeler Street School. However, if this building was

unfit for use, the first reserve was Paisley Street School. If Paisley Street was unfit then Francis Askew Boys and Girls was to be used, and if this too was damaged or destroyed, then the headquarters would move to Pickering Road School.

Division	Headquarters	Reserve Divisional Headquarters
I	Wheeler Street School	(1) Paisley Street School
		(2) Francis Askew Boys and Girls School
		(3) Pickering Road School
II	Springburn Street School	(1) Somerset Street School
		(2) Chiltern Street School
		(3) St Matthews's Parish Hall, Boulevard
III	College of Commerce	(1) St Charles' Roman Catholic School
		(2) Wawne Street School
		(3) St Thomas' Parish Hall, Campbell Street
IV	Thornesby Street School	(1) Priory Road School
		(2) Newland Avenue School
		(3) Wold Road School
V	Beverley Road School	(1) Fountain Road School
		(2) Park Road School
		(3) Lambert Street School
VI	Sidmouth Street School	(1) Hall Road School
		(2) 21st Avenue School
		(3) Endsleigh RC School, Inglemire Lane
VII	Craven Street School	(1) St Saviour's, Wilmington
		(2) Kingston Methodist Chapel, Witham
		(3) Methodist Mission Schoolroom, The Groves, Jenning Street
VIII	Mersey Street School	(1) Buckingham Street School
		(2) Cavendish Road School
		(3) Brunswick Chapel, Holderness Road
IX	Southcoates Lane School	(1) Estcourt Street School
		(2) East Park Baptist Schoolroom
		(3) Sacred Heart RC School, Southcoates Lane
X	Flinton Grove School	(1) Maybury Road School
		(2) Hopewell Road School
		(3) Marfleet School

In turn, each division had a number of Reception Centres to which people in distress could be directed after an air-raid. The centres, selected by the Air-Raid Welfare Committee were equipped to process evacuees and arrange transport to the receiving depots from which people would then be found accommodation.

In all, 92 reception centres were established in buildings ranging from Carlton Street Methodist Sunday School to the Hull and East Riding Amateur Athletic Club, Chanterlands Avenue, and 53-55 Welton Grove, Coltingham Road to Earle's Recreation Ground, Gillshill Road. The receiving depots for Hull were at Beverley, Driffield, Pocklington, Howden, North Cave and South Cave. The original plan was for evacuees from the Division One to go to North Cave, Division Two to South Cave, Division Three to Howden, Four, Five and Six Divisions to Beverley, the Seven and Eight Divisions to Driffield, Nine to Pocklington and Ten to Beverley, but this was changed, bus drivers receiving their destinations from Endike Lane School.

On page 27 of the Crash Evacuation Scheme there is an interesting instruction for teacher volunteers:

"All members of the teaching staff who have volunteered should report for duty at their appropriate duty points as soon as possible after a Blitz air-raid, whether in the daytime or during the night, or whether on a school day or during a weekend, or during a school holiday. At Divisional Headquarters, the Divisional Leaders should then arrange for the shift system to be put into operation. At Reception Centres, the staff should arrange for the shift system to be put into operation. As soon as possible after the staff on each shift has been arranged, the staff of the off-shift should go off-duty until their time for taking up duty. If time permits they will probably go home so as to secure as much rest as possible.

"If another Blitz raid is experienced, all members of the teaching staff who have volunteered for duty should again report to their duty points and the shift system again be put into operation.

It is appreciated that the circumstances at the time of an air-raid may make if difficult for an individual teacher volunteer to come to a decision as to whether it is a Blitz raid or not and hence the following illustration is given:

"Should an air-raid occur in Hull on the scale or approximately the scale of those experienced at Coventry, Sheffield and Southampton, very many houses and buildings (including schools) will be damaged, many fires will have occurred and there will be many casualties, large numbers of people will be homeless, essential services, *eg* water, electricity and gas, will not be in operation in certain districts, communications will be seriously interrupted and schools will be required for use as Reception Centres."

May 1941. The tower is all that remains of the Prudential building at the junction of King Edward and Paragon Streets. Later it had to be demolished for fear it might collapse. *Central Library Collection*

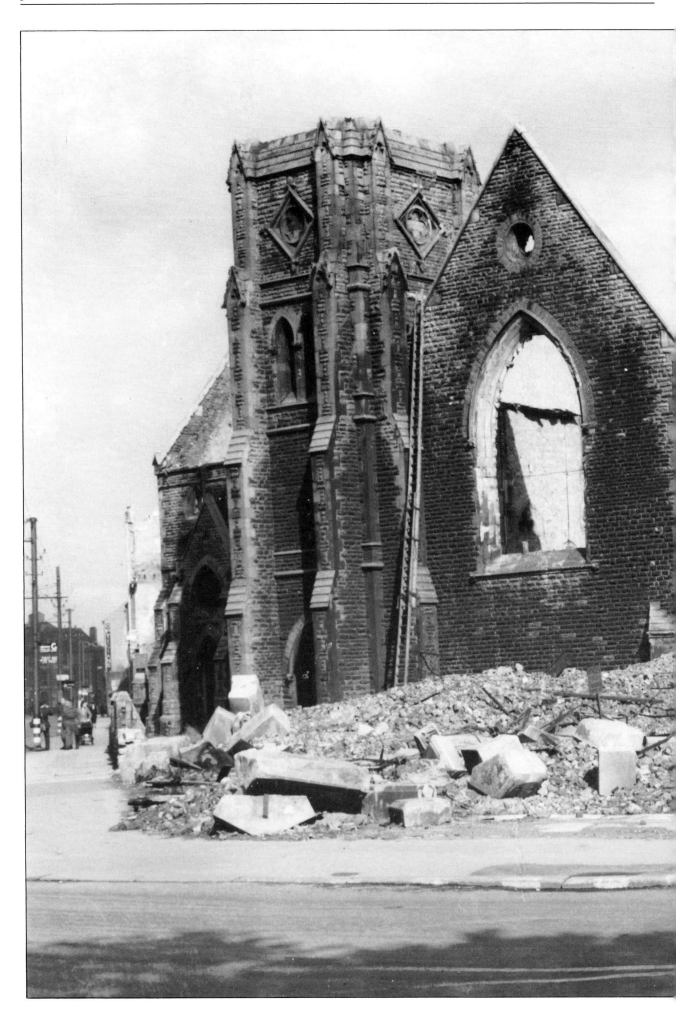

St Andrew's in Prospect Street. *Harry Cartlidge Collection.*

Above: Debris-strewn Jameson Street, May 1941. The statue of Andrew Marvell, the local seventeenth-century poet and diplomat, used to stand at the junction of Jameson Street and Bond Street. It survived the blitz unscathed but was moved to Hull Grammar School in 1963. *Central Library Collection.*

Right: The remains of Goddard, Walker & Brown. *Central Library Collection.*

Shelters

Anderson Shelters
NAMED after Sir John Anderson, Secretary of State for Home Affairs, Anderson Shelters became a familiar sight at the bottom of many a garden and examples have survived into the 1990s.

They were cheap to produce and consisted of two corrugated steel walls which met in a ridge at the top and were then bolted to sturdy rails to give the structure strength. The shelter was then 'planted' three feet (1 metre) into the ground and covered with at least 18 inches (half a metre) of earth. The entrance was protected by a steel shield and a blast wall of earth. Despite their looks, Andersons were very effective and capable of withstanding almost anything save a direct hit.

Their main drawback was that they were too small to sleep in and were prone to flooding. Initially supplied free of charge, a change in Government policy in October 1939 meant that anyone earning over £5 a week had to buy their own at prices ranging from £6.14s to £10.18s each. Production ceased in March 1940, due in part to a shortage of steel but also to the fact that the building of communal shelters had received official blessing.

Morrison Shelters
NAMED after the Minister for Home Security, Herbert Morrison, like the Anderson this type of shelter was for family use and whereas the Anderson was ideal when planted in the garden, the Morrison was definitely for use indoors. Essentially the Morrison looked like a steel table with side, of wire mesh — and yes, it could be used as a table.

Trench Shelters
THESE made their first appearance during the Czech Crisis of 1938. Most were dug in public parks and when the war eventually started, the Government issued instructions to local authorities to make the shelters more permanent by lining he sides with concrete and roofing them over with steel or concrete.

Surface Shelters
ALSO known as communal shelters, these were designed to protect up to 50 residents from a particular street or block of flats. Built of brick and cement, construction began during 1939 and continued throughout the war. However, there were problems with many of the earlier ones because of a nationwide shortage of cement resulting in little or no mortar being used. Although they looked sturdy, they were prone to collapse if hit by the pressure wave of a bomb blast. Ventilation was another problem and there was much to be desired. Even when the added luxury of a chemical toilet was provided, they could still be unbearable.

Public Shelters
SURVEYS were ordered of all town and city centres to assess how many existing cellars in shops, pubs, hotels, local authorty buildings and so on, could offer some means of protection in the event of an air-raid. Also, a number of brick and concrete surface shelters were constructed in shopping areas and although similar to the communal shelters, they could accommodate many more people.

Almost the whole of the riverside fell victim to high explosive and incendiary bombs. *Imperial War Museum.*

MINISTRY OF FOOD

YOUR NEW RATION BOOK

HOW TO REGISTER WITH THE SHOPS

The new Ration Books are now being distributed. As soon as you receive your new Book you must fill in the particulars as explained below, and then take the Book to the shops for fresh Registration. It has been found possible to allow *immediate* Registration, and the sooner you register the better.

3

ready!

coming

GUARD TIPS.

...enter a burning building or ...you have something to ...with. ...doors and windows shut ...as possible. Fire thrives ...fresh air. ...a burning room gets too ...you, shut the door as ...eat. It cuts off the air ...Besides, a door is a ...stop.

HALL RN!

HOME SECURITY

ARP rescue vehicles can be seen in the background of this photograph of Waterloo/St Paul's Streets, May 1941. *Central Library Collection.*

Newland Avenue. *Central Library Collection.*

The scene of devastation at Watt Street, 11 May 1941. *Central Library Collection.*

Trolley buses back in service following the clearing of King Edward Street. Notice the sign for the public shelter and the white bands around posts. *Central Library Collection.*

Wellington Lane. *Central Library Collection.*

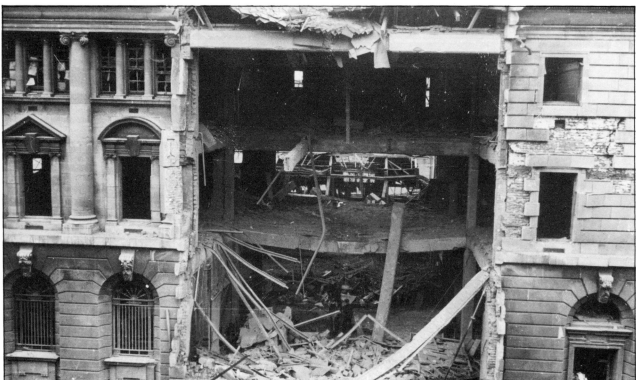

All Will Be Trained to Fire Guard

COMPULSORY training for fire guards was announced by Miss Ellen Wilkinson, Parliamentary Secretary to the Ministry of Home Security, in a speech at Newcastle yesterday.

The scheme will apply to fire guards serving under the local authority and also to those at business and Government premises.

But the training will not be an extra liability, Miss Wilkinson pointed out. It will take place during the 48 hours of part-time service a month.

The recent "Baedeker" raids, said Miss Wilkinson, had shown very clearly how vital a part fire guards could play when an incendiary attack was made on a town.

"The National Fire Service," she went on, "naturally concentrate on the big fires that break out, and it then depends on the fire guards alone whether other serious fires start or whether this is prevented."

Makeshift barbers' shop, whilst clearing bomb damage.

Visit by their Majesties King George VI and Queen Elizabeth to Hull on 6 August 1941.

Winston Churchill visits Hull's bombed areas. *Imperial War Museum.*

The Lord Mayor, Councillor Sydney Smith, visits evacuated children at Hatfield Modern School, 3 September 1941.

The Lord Mayor's visit continues this time at Gate Burton Hall, Lincolnshire.

Evacuated children at Holme-on-Spalding Moor.

Sergeant Major R.A.Drysdale and Battery Sergeant-Major J.Clayton, both of Guelph, Ontario, Canada, are on hand to present the citizens of Hull with this mobile canteen on 13 August 1941.

Princes Avenue/Park Grove in 1941. *Central Library Collection.*

Dated 5 August 1942. ARP vehicles parked up prior to the commencement of a major exercise in the Grindell Street area. *Central Library Collection.*

Listening out for anyone trapped under the rubble. *Central Library Collection.*

August 1942. Hull Civil Defence Rescue Service developed a system for moving large slabs of debris. The 'Hull lift' was used at the training school at Pearson Park. *Central Library Collection.*

Opposite page and above: These pictures show an area cleared of debris within 72 hours. *Central Library Collection.*

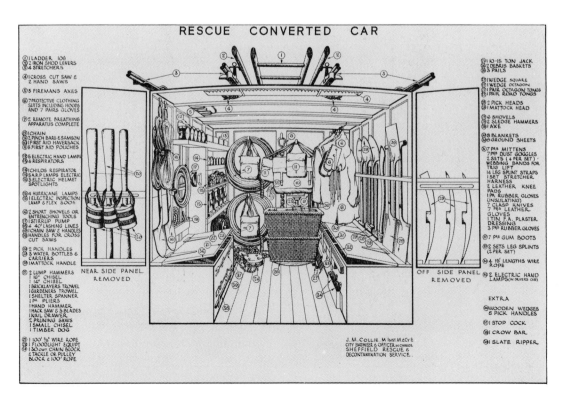

Left: Standard rescue vehicle developed by Sheffield Rescue and Decontamination Service for use nationwide.

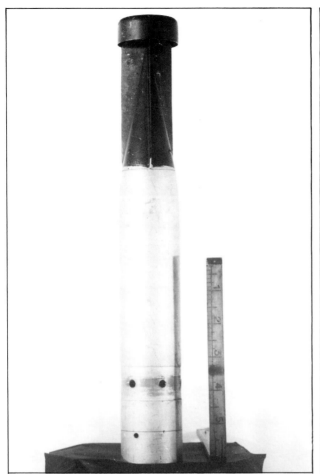 

Left: Incendiary bomb; the rule gives an idea as to the size of these very effective weapons. *Right:* The sort of damage that even one incendiary could so easily inflict if not tackled straight away.

Royal Engineers excavate a trench in an attempt to reach an unexploded and possibly delayed-action 1,000kg bomb.

Rescue work in progress in May 1942. *Central Library Collection.*

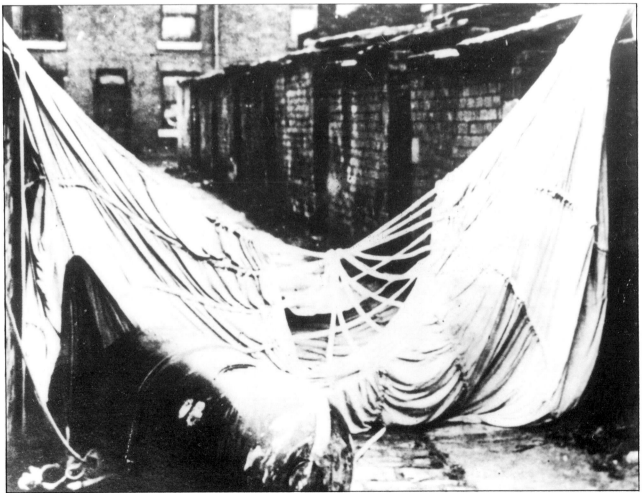

Parachute mine down between two rows of houses.

Two views of the scene at Southcoates Lane railway bridge, destroyed by a bomb in July 1943. *Central Library Collection.*

Damage to the docks. *Harry Cartlidge Collection.*

Junkers JU88A-5 of 3/KG30 shot down by Sergeant McNay of 73 Squadron during an attack on Driffield aerodrome. The plane crash landed and the crew of four were all captured unhurt, 15 August 1940.

Above: Another photo of the Junkers JU88A-5 wreck.

Right and top right: Junkers UV88A-1 of 8/KG30 was shot down by Hurricanes of 302 (Polish) Squadron and crashed at Patrington. Of the crew, Unteroffizier Willi Rautenberg was killed and Oberfeldwebel Kruczinski severely wounded but died two days later.

The War at Sea

IT was the Americans who first coined the phrase 'Phoney War' for the period up to the German invasion of Norway in April 1940. But there was nothing phoney about the war at sea, a war from which thousands of ships and tens of thousands of sailors would never return.

The war at sea would bring out the very best and the very worst in both sides. It would be a war of countless tales of courage and determination and of untold acts of bravery because there were no survivors left to tell. It would be a war of lucky escapes and frightful disasters, of appalling conditions and brilliant seamanship, of magnaminity and downright cold blooded brutality.

There was determination like that of the crew of the *Imperial Transport* who succeeded in bringing the stern section of their ship home after it had been cut in half by a torpedo. There was the sacrifice made by the crew of the armed merchant cruiser *Jervis Bay* in engaging the German armoured ship *Admiral Scheer* so that the convoy they were escorting might gain a few precious minutes in which to scatter and make their escape.

Then there was the *San Demetrio*, an oil tanker set ablaze by the *Scheer's* gunfire and abandoned by her crew, only to be reboarded later whilst still white hot and in danger of blowing up, to be brought home with the bare minimum of navigational aids. And there was the tragedy of the evacuee ships taking children to safety in North America. The bewildered children from the *City of Simla*, the courage of the young survivors of the *Volendam*, who when asked if they wanted to try and cross the Atlantic again shouted, 'Yes!' and set off again in the ill-fated *City of Benares*.

Hull, Britain's third port in the 1930s, would naturally play an important role in the war, as would her merchant ships and fishing vessels. Local fishing companies made their first contribution to the build-up of the Royal Navy in 1935, when during the Abyssinia crisis a number of modern trawlers including the *Cape Warwick, Cape Finisterre, Cape Guardafui, Kingston Coral, Kingston Cyanite* and the *Lord Brentford* were purchased to reinforce the fleet's anti-submarine and minesweeping capabilities. Before war was declared, the Navy purchased another batch of Hull trawlers including the *Lord Dawson, Lord Hewart, Cape Duner, Cape Barfleur* and the *St Irene*.

At the end of World War One nearly 600 trawlers were in service or under construction for the Royal Navy, the majority based on three commercial designs, Smith's Docks Castle Class, Cochrane's Mersey Class and Hall Russell's Strath Class. With the ending of hostilities, of the 215 trawlers under construction, 82 were cancelled, the remainder being completed for commerical owners.

Between the wars, the Navy's trawler force was so

HMS Wells (XUSS Tillman) on coastal escort duty off the Yorkshire coast. The destroyer was one of 50 acquired from the United States in return for leases on Caribbean bases.

run-down that by 1939 only three Castles, 14 Merseys and one Strath remained, together with four Axe Class, six Bassett Class and the 40 vessels purchased since 1935.

From August 1939, the Admiralty began to requisition commerical fishing vessels for use on anti-submarine, minesweeping, boom defence and depot ship duties, resulting in no less than 125 Castles, 30 Merseys and 75 Straths rejoining the fleet. Even so, the Navy was still desperately short of auxiliary warships and additional requisitions were made, involving another 322 trawlers plus drifters and a handful of whalers by the end of September 1939.

In October, another 24 trawlers were taken over, followed in November by 144, and 28 in December. The age and tonnage varied tremendously from the brand-new Hull trawler *Akita* of 314 gross tonnes, to the venerable *City of Aberdeen* of 194 gross tonnes built in 1898. The oldest drifters requisitioned during this period appears to have been the *Betty Inglis* of 1895, although the 1885-built *Welcome* was called up during 1940.

By the end of 1939, the bulk of Hull's modern deep-sea trawler fleet was in Admiralty hands and so were most of the crews. St Andrew's Fish Dock had closed down. For the few remaining commerical boats still sailing out of the Humber, the war brought new dangers with drifting mines and the Luftwaffe rarely passing up on the opportunity to bomb and strafe. But on occasion the ships flying the Red Duster bit back.

On 2 August 1940, the well-known Hull trader *SS Highlander* steamed into port proudly displaying the wreckage of a Heinkel 115 seaplane across her stern. The 1,000-tonne steamer had been attacked, the enemy dropping its bombs then turning to rake the vessel with machine-gun fire. Whilst doing so, the German pilot got just a little too close to the *Highlander*, where the gunners were holding their fire until the last possible second. The pilot never knew what hit him, his 'plane nose-diving in flames into the sea about 100 yards astern of the steamer.

Whilst the gunners were still celebrating their success, another aircraft, the Heinkel 115, suddenly appeared on the scene and attacked. The aircraft made several passes over the steamer, dropping its bombs, all of which missed. As the aircraft circled to attack once more, it was hit and lost height. The port wing clipped the *Highlander's* port lifeboat, the impact swinging the 'plane round and down on to the poop deck where it burst into flames. Luckily the crew managed to put the fire out. There were no survivors from either aircraft.

But at sea, it was often the case that there were no survivors. A torpedoed ammunition ship, aviation-spirit tanker or petro-chemical carrier was liable to instantaneously disintegrate, scattering debris over several miles, whilst heavily-laden ore carriers had a propensity for sinking like a stone. Ageing tramp steamers were prone to sinking within seconds of being torpedoed and many ships simply sailed from port, neither they or their crews ever to be heard from again.

The Hull trawler *Crystal* was mined off Scarborough on 26 June 1942. *Harry Cartlidge Collection.*

Merchant seamen on a gunnery course. October 1939.

Stern-chaser being fitted to a merchantman in October 1939. By the end of the war many merchant ships carried a considerable anti-aircraft/anti-ship armament.

When Elder Dempster's *Accra* was torpedoed on 26 July 1940, fourth officer John Thomas of Cottingham Road and the other 450 survivors had just under an hour to get clear before the ship finally slipped beneath the waves, after developing a list to starboard.

Of the sinking, Mr Thomas said, "One of the many brave deeds I saw performed was by a man who, seeing a passenger had fallen overboard and was in danger of being caught by the propellers, despite the extreme danger, slid down the painter and fastened a rope around the passenger. He was hauled in but, unfortunately, was dead."

Other vessels had surprisingly lucky escapes. The *Empire Haywood Stanhope*, on a voyage from Seville in neutral Spain with a cargo of marmalade and oranges, had been sabotaged by a German agent who had planted a number of delayed action bombs in the crates. The bombs went off but the explosions were muffled by the now soft and sticky cargo. When the ship arrived in the UK it was decided that all the cases would have to be opened and the cargo discharged down chutes into lighters. In doing so many oranges fell overboard, resulting in a scramble by the locals for the normally unobtainable delights.

Towards the end of 1941, the Merchant Navy became subject of an Essential Work Order and although men could no longer leave the service, they were guaranteed wages between voyages and statutory leave. Before the war, pay had been abysmal, an able-seaman earning as little as £10 a month but working anything up to a 110 hours a week. On top of this, accomodation was often primitive and dirty, the only space a man might call his own was that occupied by his bunk in the soot-filled atmosphere of the bogey-stored forecastle.

An officer's accommodation on the average tramp steamer was a little better. He might have his own cabin but it was usually spartan and cramped, only the captain's would be panelled and only the captain would have the exclusive use of private washing facilities. In 1938, the Medical Officer for Hull and Goole found that 374 British-registered vessels inspected by him that year had dirty quarters and another 105 gave cause for concern.

But if the pay in the Merchant Navy had been abysmal, the skippers still fishing commercially stood to make a fortune. Prices had rocketed. In 1941 a stone of haddock could fetch 18s compared to its pre-war price of 4s. At Fleetwood a 10st-box of plaice could fetch up to £19, five times the peacetime figure. The smallest size of fish, usually a give-away at 5s a box, was now making £8.10s. Hake made £10 a box, the biggest size of fish being £1 10s each.

Skippers returning from a trip to Icelandic waters could make at least £500 from one voyage and their crew would double or treble their normal wages.

For the trawler crews in Royal Navy service, it was Royal Navy rates of pay — and the Navy did not pay danger money. The larger and faster trawlers of the Hull fleet were usually fitted out for anti-submarine duties, the older vessels for minesweeping. Armament varied according to availability and function. An anti-submarine trawler would mount a 4in gun, failing that a six-pounder or 12-pounder. Minesweeping

Mr Roy Miller arrives at Hull Paragon after being released from *Altmark,* the German prison ship.

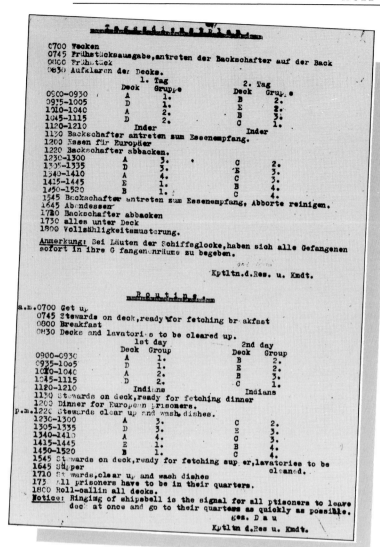

The notice of daily routine for prisoners aboard *Altmark*.

trawlers usually carried a 12-pounder but had to make do with whatever was available.

Anti-aircraft protection also varied ranging from 20mm Bofors guns on Naval trawlers to 5in machine-guns or Lewis guns for the requisitioned boats. By the end of the war, virtually all trawlers still in service with the Navy were equipped with a 4in-gun and several 20mm Bofors guns.

Despite the requisitioning of trawlers which continued through 1940, the Navy was still short of ships. Orders for new construction were placed based on the Admiralty-designed Bassett Class, of which the Dance, Tree, Isles and Shakespearian Classes were all variants. Commercial designs were also pressed into service. Hall Russell's *Star of Orkney* of 1936 was used as the basis for the Round Table Class. Cochrane's *Gulfoss* of 1929 led to the Fish Class, and Cook, Welton and Gemmill's *Barnett* of 1937 inspired the Hill Class.

From early 1941, Cook, Welton and Gemmill took over the building of Naval trawlers from Smith's Dock, so as the latter could concentrate on the construction of corvettes and frigates. Cook, Welton and Gemmill's first Naval trawlers were the *Birch* and *Blackthorne*, both launched in November 1939. During 1940, they launched the Dance Class anti-submarine trawlers *Gavotte* and *Hornpipe*, together with a quartet of minesweeping vessles *Hamlet*, *Horatio*, *Juliet* and *Laertes*.

November 1940 saw the launch of the *Arran;* the first of 59 Isles Class to be built by Cook, Welton and Gemmell. The following year the first of eight Hill Class took to the water and between November 1942 and July 1944, nine Military Class were launched.

From the middle of 1944, the Admiralty slowly began to release requisitioned trawlers for return to their owners. For the Grimsby and Hull fleets, the release was a gradual process throughout 1944 and for much of 1945. The *Kingston Onyx* returned in September 1944, the *Lord Darling* two months later.

The pilots of 220 Squadron, Coastal Command who helped locate the *Altmark*. The hunt for the *Altmark* began on 16 February 1940, when agents indicated that she was off Norway. After an early morning briefing, three Hudsons, of 220 Squadron took off from Thornaby, locating the ship some two hours later. The Hudsons continued to shadow *Altmark* until 1400hrs, when ships of the Royal Navy closed in, intercepted and boarded her.

In March 1945, the *Kingston Chrysoberyl* and the *Kingston Crystal* were amongst those released. By the end of September, the *Arctic Hunter, Cape Melville, Cape Nyemetski, Cape Palliser, Kingston Cyanite, Kingston Coral, Northern Sky, Northern Spray* and *Northern Wave* were back in the Humber.

The process went on into 1946 and a number of former Naval trawlers were sold to Hull and Grimsby owners. The veteran *Armentiers* became the *Arctic Rovers,* the *Cornelian* became the commerical trawler *Lincoln City,* the *Syringa* returned to Hull as the *Cape Kanin* — her original name until purchased by the Admiralty in 1935.

Then there were those that would never return.

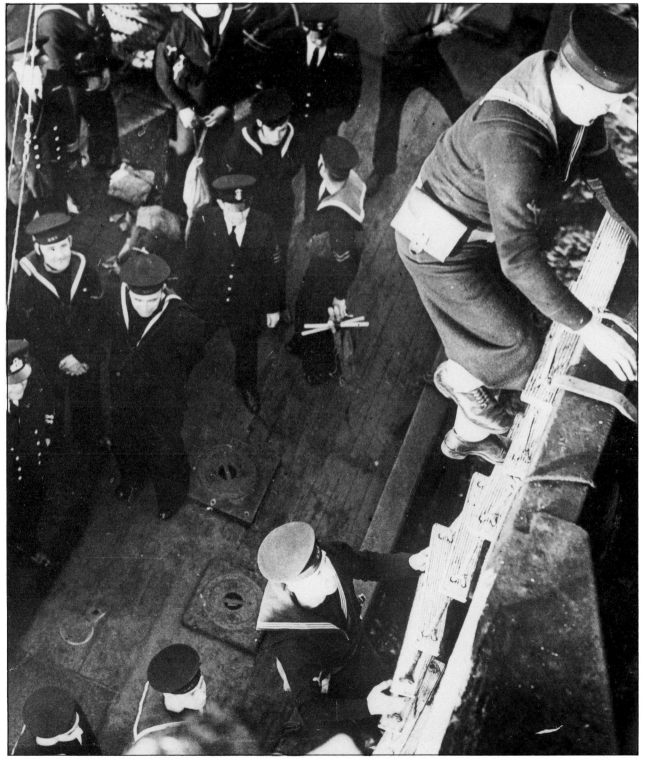

Armed sailors from a trawler on contraband control board a steamer in the search for raw materials bound for Germany, either directly or indirectly via a neutral county.

The continuing search for contraband.

Naval officers discuss the situation off the Humber. They were responsible for
the operational deployment of patrol vessels operating out of Hull and Grimsby.
Imperial War Museum.

The motor vessel *Groenland* at Hull. When Norway fell to the Germans, a number of Norwegian merchant ships made their way to the Humber to continue the fight. *Harry Cartlidge Collection.*

The Hull trawler *Lord Hailsham* of 443 gross tonnes was built in 1934 and requisitioned by the Admiralty in August 1939. She was sunk by an E-boat in the Channel on 27 February 1943.

The *Kingston Amber* seen on an anti-submarine patrol from the deck of the requisitioned Grimsby trawler *Northern Gem*.

The *Kingston Olivine* requisitioned in August 1939 for anti-submarine and minesweeping duties. She was the adopted ship of Hemsworth Urban District. *Imperial War Museum.*

Above: Crew members of the *Kingston Olivine*. Showing *(left to right)*, Leading Seaman J.F.Saunders, Seamen C.Taylor and John McCartney. *Imperial War Museum.*

Below: Officers of the *Kingston Olivine (left to right).* Lieutenant T.Maxwell RNVR (first Lieutenant); Lieutenant Evers RANVR (the commanding officer); Sub-Lieutenant F.Pearson RNVR. *Imperial War Museum.*

A FEW
CARELESS WORDS
MAY END IN THIS—
Many lives were lost in the last war through careless talk
Be on your guard! Don't discuss movements of ships or troops

Shackling tanks to the sides of a hold aboard the *Cape Corso* at Hull in March 1943.

On the night of Wednesday 22 November 1939, a German aircraft was seen to drop an object by parachute into the sea off Shoeburyness but within the low-water line. At team from *HMS Vernon* were sent to investigate and discovered that the object was a magnetic mine, the first to fall into British hands. The picture was not released for publication until May 1943.

Even Shackleton's old ship *Quest* was requisitioned. She served from November 1940 until October 1945 with the Royal Norwegian Navy.

Built by Cooke, Welton and Gemmell, HMS *Sapper* was one of nine anti-submarine trawlers comprising the Military class. All built by CW & G, the others were *Bombardier, Coldstreamer, Fusilier, Grenadier, Guardsman, Home Guard, Lancer* and *Royal Marine*. In 1946 *Sapper* became *Cape Gloucester*, a commercial trawler. *Harry Cartlidge Collection*.

Icelandic trawlers in Hull. Also in the picture is the *Eday*, a minesweeping trawler of the Isles Class built by Cochrane. *Harry Cartlidge Collection.*

Above and below: The dock office, where Harry Cartlidge worked, heavily protected by sandbags.

Ellerman Wilson's *City of Karachi* was bombed and sunk at Volo, Greece, on 13 April 1941.

Ellerman
Wilson's
*City of Lin-
coln* was
damaged in
an air-raid
on Grand
Harbour,
Malta, on
23 March
1941. Refit-
ted, she
returned to
the war
only to
become a
casualty
again. On
19 February
1945 she
was mined,
300° eight
cables from
No 14 buoy
off the
Humber.

Blockade Runners

IN the early evening of 23 October 1943, five motor gunboats (MGBs) slipped their moorings and proceeded down the Humber and into the North Sea. Once clear of the coastal minefield they altered course for the Skagerrak and increased speed: the first mission of 'Operation Bridford' was on.

By July 1940, it was becoming ever more apparent that unless supplies of Swedish ball-bearings and machine tools could be maintained, Britain's war effort would be seriously undermined.

The man chosen to undertake the task was George Binney, a 40-year-old metallurgist-cum-explorer, who had been despatched to Sweden by the British Iron and Steel Federation at the start of the war, but who was also well-connected with the twilight world of Military and Naval intelligence and had links with the Ministry of Economic Warfare.

In January 1941, Binney organized the break-out of five Norwegian merchant ships interned in Swedish ports with around 25,000 tonnes of highly desirable engineering equipment, machine tools and raw materials sitting in their holds. The operation was a complete success and, suitably encouraged, Binney organized a second break-out involving ten ships. It was a disaster, only two ships making it to the UK, two turning back to Sweden and six being sunk.

The neutral Swedes banned interned merchant ships from attempting to break-out, but they were agreeable to vessels sailing from Britain to pick up cargoes, so the plan was developed whereby converted MGBs flying the Red Ensign would make the runs.

On 25 April 1943, the Admiralty allocated five MGBs to the operation. Built by Camper and Nicholson, the boats were 117ft long, had a beam of 20.25ft and a draught of only 3.75ft to 4.15ft. Each boat was powered by three Davey Paxman Ricardo 16-cylinder diesels, each developing 1,000hp, giving a speed of 23 knots. Cargo capacity was increased by gutting the accommodation areas both fore and aft. Defensive armament comprised 20mm Oerlikons and Vickers machine-guns.

The boats were to be based at Hull under the management of Ellerman Wilson, and Binney personally selected the crews, 80 per cent of whom lived in and around Hull. Binney also chose the names of the vessels *Hopewell* (XMGB504); *Nonsuch* (XMGB505); *Gay Viking* (XMGB506); *Gay Corsair* (XMGB507) and *Master Standfast* (XMGB508).

The basic operation was for the MGBs to pass through the Skagerrak during the hours of darkness. After entering Swedish territorial waters they would head for Lysekil. The return trip would also be carried

Blockade runners at sea. *Hopewell* seen from *Nonsuch*.

Inside the engine room of the *Nonsuch*.

Some of *Gay Corsair's* crew with their skipper, Captain Bob Tanton.

out at night so that by daybreak they would be well into the North Sea and air-cover from the RAF.

On the first run, only one MGB reached Sweden. The *Gay Viking* had suffered engine trouble and had been left behind as the other four boats pressed on. However, during the 27th, repeated sightings of German aircraft led Binney to believe that the mission had been compromised so he ordered his four boats to return to the Humber.

In the meantime, blissfully unaware that her consorts had turned for home, *Gay Viking* was again underway and making for the Skagerrak at best possible speed. By 0400, the MGB was in Swedish territorial waters, Captain Whitfield bringing her in to Lysekil shortly after 0700. *Gay Viking* put to sea for the return leg on the evening of 29 October, arriving at Immingham on the morning of 31st.

The flotilla's first casualty on the 1,200 mile run came on 2 November 1943, when the *Master Standfast*, commanded by Captain George Holdsworth, was intercepted and captured by the German patrol vessel *VP1606*. Captain Holdsworth later died of wounds at Frederickshaun, Denmark, and a number of the crew were made prisoners-of-war.

By the summer of 1944, Binney's navy had brought over 340 tonnes of desperately-needed ball-bearings and engineering equipment, but the short summer nights prevented any more trips. When winter returned, the blockade runners were again at sea, this time involved in covert operations for the SOE. On 6 February 1945, the *Gay Viking*, *Hopewell* and *Nonsuch* put to sea on 'Operation Moonshine' to deliver small arms and ammunition to the Dutch Resistance. It was during the operation that the flotilla's second loss occurred when the *Gay Viking* sank after being in collision with the *Hopewell*. On the return trip, the *Nonsuch* and *Hopewell* brought back over 60 tonnes of high-grade steel.

The *Hopewell* heads for home across the North Sea following a successful run.

Naval Warships Auxiliaries lost off the Humber

Name	Type	Fate
Benvolio	Minesweeping Trawler	Mined 23.2.1940
Princess Victoria	Auxiliary Minelayer	Mined 19.5.1940
Dervish	Minesweeping Trawler	Mined 9.9.1940
ML109	Motor Launch	Mined 30.10.1940
Gael	Harbour Defence Patrol Craft	Mined 24.11.1940
ML111	Motor Launch	Mined 25.11.1940
Manx Prince	Minesweeping Trawler	Mined 28.11.1940
Calverton	Minesweeping Trawler	Mined 29.11.1940
Cortina	Minesweeping Trawler	Collision 7.12.1940
St Cyrus	Fleet Tug	Mined 22.1.1941
Luda Lady	Minesweeping Trawler	Mined 22.1.1941
Remillo	Auxiliary Patrol Vessel	Mined 27.2.1941
St Donats	Minesweeping Trawler	Collision 1.3.1941
Lord Selbourne	Auxiliary Patrol Vessel	Mined 31.3.1941
Bahram	Harbour Defence Patrol Craft	Mined 3.4.1941
Othello	Contraband Control	Mined 11.4.1941
Susarion	Auxiliary Patrol Vessel	Bombed 7.5.1941
Silicia	Minesweeping Trawler	Mined 8.5.1941
Pintail	Sloop	Mined 10.6.1941
Strathborve	Minesweeping Trawler	Mined 6.9.1941
Corfield	Mine Destructor Vessel	Mined 8.9.1941
MASB30	Motor Anti-Submarine Boat	Fouled boom & sank 14.12.1941
Henriette	Minesweeping Trawler (Free-French)	Mined 26.12.1941
Loch Alsh	Minesweeping Trawler	Mined 30.1.1942
Cape Spartel	Minesweeping Trawler	Bombed 2.2.1942
Cloughton Wyke	Minesweeping Trawler	Bombed 2.2.1942
Meror	Minesweeping Trawler	Mined 3.10.1943
Cap D'Antifer	Minesweeping Trawler (Free-French)	Torpedoed by E-Boat 13.2.1944

Wartime posters photographed by Harry Cartlidge.

Wartime poster photographed by Harry Cartlidge, and the LNER vans which have their running boards and mud guards painted white as an aid during the black-out.

Hull Air Training Corps dance at the Beverley Road Baths, February 1941.

Hull Air Cadets visit a bomber station and are given a look over a Stirling bomber. In the picture above, Cadet Norman Bryant, aged 15, from Hull, is shown the mysteries of the rear turret of a Wellington by Sergeant Owens of Melbourne, Australia. *Imperial War museum.*

Cadets examining an engine.

Cadet gets to grips with the controls of a training aircraft. *Imperial War Museum.*

Hull ATC cadets pose for the camera. *Imperial War Museum.*

Cadets and regulars way-lay the NAAFI van. *Imperial War Museum.*

Lord Harewood with Squadron Leader Beard MC, and other RAF and ATC officers, inspect the kit of Hull ATC cadets. *Imperial War Museum*

Small boys and dad's delight. A Spitfire in Hull and not in the air: the centrepiece of a Battle of Britain/recruiting exhibition. *Harry Cartlidge Collection.*

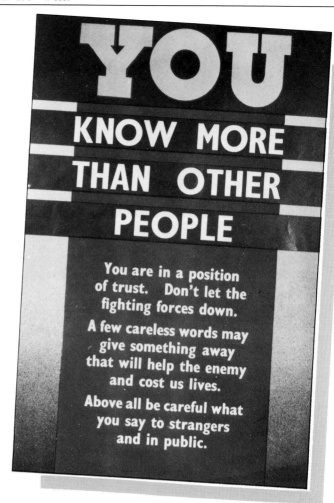

Rifle drill for Bren-gun carrier crews of the East
Riding Yeomanry, 15 February 1940.

Above: Dispatch riders of the East Riding Yeomanry attempt a racing start during an exercise in February 1940.

Left: Major W.Holtby, commanding C Squadron, East Riding Yeomanry, briefs troop commanders during the Normandy offensive. Photograph taken by Sergeant Mapham on 28 June 1944.

King George VI inspects the East Riding Yeomanry at Colchester in October 1940. Photograph taken by Mr Puttnam.

East Riding Yeo-
manry   tanks
warm up prior to
going into action
on 28 June 1944
in support of
infantry of 9 Bri-
gade, 3 Division.

Sergeant Laing
snapped   these
East Riding Yeo-
manrymen pre-
paring an even-
ing meal prior to
taking over Buf-
falo amphibious
vehicles for the
Rhine crossing.

The 2nd Battalion in the Maginot Line at St Francois, 4 February 1940.

Left: The East Yorkshire Regiment (The Duke of York's own) was raised in 1685 as the 15th Foot and fought under General Wolf at Louisberg and Quebec. The local Territorial battalion, the 4th, was sent to France with the BEF and took part in the withdrawal through Dunkirk. In 1941, the 4th Battalion served in Egypt, Cyprus and Palestine before being captured in Libya. The 5th Battalion was raised in 1939 as a duplicate of the 4th. It served with the 50th Infantry Division in France and later fought at El Alamein and in North Africa.

Below: Road block manned by 2nd Battalion at St Francis, February 1940.

Above: Field Marshall
Montgomery visits the
5th Battalion, East
Yorkshire Regiment
after its return to Britain
from Sicily.

Right: Picture taken by
Sergeant Ackland on 26
August 1942. A shell
bursts in front of a Bren-
gun carrier belonging to
the 5th Battalion.

Bren-gun carriers of the 5th Battalion trundle along a Sicilian road.

Shells fall in and around the 2nd Battalion's positions on the Normandy beach-head.

The 2nd Battalion start to move inland.

Members of the 2nd Battalion at Venray. Note that the military censor has removed shoulder flashes from battledress tunics.

Counter patrol by 2nd Battalion on 21 March 1945. The company commander was Major C.K.King DSO, the patrol was led by Corporal E.David. The object of a counter patrol was to counteract German intelligence gathering patrols. Before setting off, the men handed in letters, pay books and anything that would identify them if captured. Photograph taken by Lieutenant P.T.Hanford.

D Company, 2nd Battalion, 21 March 1945. Time for a chat and a fag, perhaps a brew before setting out on another counter patrol. Photograph taken by Lieutenant P.T.Hanford.

The 1st Battalion advance towards Rangoon.

MILK BAR

"NOW! WHERE'S THAT BLOKE HITLER!!"

This photograph was taken in Hull, where a bombed area had been converted to a vehicle proving ground for the army. Here HRH The Princess Royal watches as a jeep is put through its paces.

ATS drivers besiege the 'tuck shop' following pay parade.

Just where did all those scarves, socks and balaclavas knitted by tens of thousands of ladies go to? The bulk of them,
if not sent direct to a serviceman, finished up here at the Army Comforts Depot at Reading from where they were dispatched
to units at home and overseas.

In 1942 the ATS got its own Military Police. Here Junior Commandant Jill MacDermott inspects the Red Corps before they go on duty.

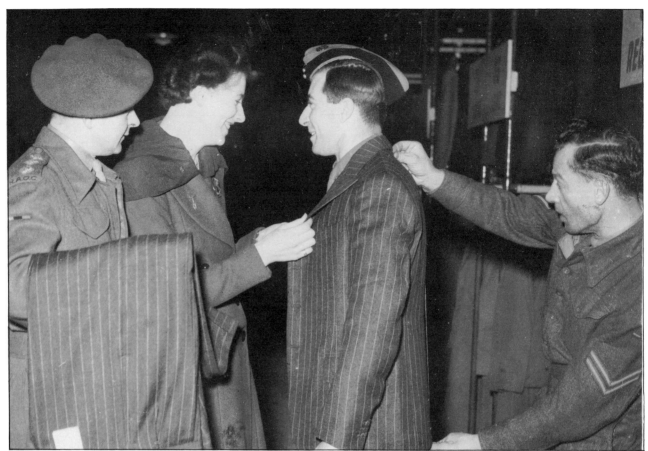

Sergeant Peter Donaldson, watched by his fianceé, Miss Irene Walker, is measured for his demob suit at the Army Clothing
Depot in February 1945. The army valued the whole outfit, suit, shirt, two collars, a tie, two pairs of socks, a pair of
shoes, raincoat, hat and shaving tackle and a toothbrush at £11. On the black market it was possible to get £20 or more
for the outfit because the buyer stood to save 56 clothing coupons. The annual clothing ration in 1945 was 48 coupons.
A man's suit in Utility cloth took 24 coupons, a work shirt five coupons plus 7s 9d, men's trousers five coupons plus
16s 6d, ladies' woollen frocks 11 coupons plus 73s 9d and children's gaberdine raincoats 12 coupons plus 56s 3d.

Above and opposite page (bottom): Children's parties, mainly in the street, occasionally in a church hall or school, were the highlight for many during the May 1945 VE celebrations. One of the interesting phenomina of the parties was the sudden appearance of long-missed goodies such as jellies, tinned fruit and the like. Some streets waited until VJ Day (Victory over Japan) in August before holding parties, many celebrated both.

As well as parties, there were celebration bonfires and some streets even managed to get their hands on a few fireworks, which had been officially banned since 1939.

Normality returns to Hull. Although most of the trawler fleet was still serving with the Royal Navy in May 1945, these Danish Seine netters provided a regatta-like atmosphere. Note the bombed-out buildings in the background. *Harry Cartlidge Collection.*

Troops disembark from the *Empire Rapier. Harry Cartlidge Collection.*

Riverside quay showing the sections of Mulberry Harbour in use. *Harry Cartlidge Collection.*

Central Library Collection

Flashback to 1941 with a visit by HRH the Princess Royal to the Guides and Brownies at the Newland Orphan Home.

"For what we are about to receive." Young 'volunteers', towels at the ready, are about to go where no one from Hull had gone before — into the Lifebuoy emergency bath services' mobile bath house. These units were deployed into bombed-out areas as were Rinso's mobile laundries.

Fact File

1939
24 March
Britain and France guarantee Poland's frontier.
3 April
Hitler orders *Wehrmacht* to prepare invasion of Poland.
August
Requisitioning of Hull trawler fleet by Admiralty begins.
20 August
Russia and Germany sign trade agreement.
24 August
Britain calls up military reservists and ARP workers put on alert.
29 August
Hitler announces he will negotiate if Poland sends emissary to Berlin by noon the following day. His demand is rejected.
30 August
Warships of Royal Navy proceed to war stations.
31 August
Hitler orders invasion of Poland to begin at dawn on 1 September.
1 September
Invasion of Poland begins. Italy declares non-belligerent status. Scandinavia and Baltic States declare neutrality. Evacuation of British towns and cities begins.
2 September
Eire declares neutrality.
3 September
Britain and France declare war on Germany. India, Australia and New Zealand declare war on Germany. Belgium proclaims neutrality.
SS *Athenia* torpedoed and sunk by U-boat in contravention of a direct order from Hitler.
4 September
Advance units of British Expeditionary Force (BEF) arrive in France. 3.20am sees Hull's first air-raid alert.
10 September
Canada declares war on Germany.
17 September
Russia invades Poland.
27 September
Poland surrenders.
29 September
Russia and Germany formally divide Poland between them.
6 October
Hitler offers peace settlement to Britain and France.
11 October
BEF strength in France 158,000 troops.
12 October
Hitler's peace offer rejected.
14 October
Battleship *Royal Oak* torpedoed and sunk in Scapa Flow.
8 November
Assassination attempt on Hitler fails.
22 November
Trawler *Kingston Arogonite* lost.

30 November
Following dispute over status of islands in the Baltic, Russia invades Finland.
3 December
Conscription of all males aged 19-41 introduced in Britain. Females aged 20-30 are required to join women's auxiliary forces or do essential war work.
29 December
Finns inflict crushing defeat on Red Army at Suommusalmi.

1940
8 January
Rationing of basic food stuffs begins in Britain. Finns defeat Red Army at Karelin.
11 February
Red Army launches massive offensive against Finland.
17 February
Further evacuations of British towns and cities.
23 February
Minesweeping Trawler *Benvolio* mined off the Humber.
12 March
Russo-Finnish war ends.
29 March
Russia declares her neutrality in the European war.
8 April
Germany invades Norway and Denmark. End of 'Phoney War'.
10 May
Germany invades Low Countries.
13 May
Germany invades France. Liege falls.
18 May
Antwerp falls to the Germans.
26 May
Evacuation of Allied troops from beaches of Dunkirk begins.
10 June
Neville Chamberlain resigns as Prime Minister and is replaced by Winston Churchill. Italy declares war on Britain and France.
14 June
Anthony Eden calls for volunteers to join the Local Defence Force (Home Guard).
16 June
Germans enter Paris.
22 June
Armistice between France and Germany.
1 July
Daylight raid by single aircraft on oil storage tanks at Saltend, one tank set on fire, intruder shot down.
2 July
Hitler orders invasion of Britain.
19 July
Peace terms offered to Britain by Hitler.
15 August
Luftwaffe launch all-out assault on RAF.
25 August
Hull's first fatalities in an air-raid, six people killed.

27/28 August
Hull raided again. Maternity home on Hedon Road hit but no serious casualties.
7 September
London blitz begins.
17 September
Evacuation ship *City of Benares* torpedoed and sunk by U-boat.
28 October
Italy invades Greece but suffers series of military setbacks.
30 October
Chamberlain resigns from the Government.
1 November
Daylight raid on Hull, one person killed, eight seriously injured.
8 November
Minor raid on Hull, no fatalities reported but two people seriously injured.
11 November
Minor raid on Hull, no fatalities reported.
14-15 November
Coventry devastated in an 11-hour raid.
30 November-7 December
Hull War Weapons Week.

1941
21 January
Daily Worker closed down under the Defence Regulations.
Tobruk falls to British and Australian troops.
12 February
German troops land in North Africa.
22-23 February
Minor attack on Hull. 32 tonnes HE and incendiaries dropped. 12 people killed.
13 March
Sharp attack on Hull results in 38 killed and 790 seriously injured.
Dornier DO17 shot over Hull, crashing into sea off Skegness.
31 March
Heaviest attack on Hull to date, 52 killed and 72 seriously injured. ARP Control Centre hit and Infirmary badly damaged.
5 April
Germans forced to intervene in Greece to save Italians from defeat.
8 April
HRH The Princess Royal visits Hull.
15 April
Community shelter in Holderness Road takes direct hit from parachute mine leaving 60 dead and many seriously injured.
20 April
Greeks surrender
7-8 May
Major raid on Hull due to aircraft being diverted en route from their primary target of Liverpool.
8-9 May
Major raid on Hull due to aircraft being diverted en route from their primary target of Sheffield.
10 May
Rudolf Hess lands in Scotland. Last and worst of London's blitz raids with 1,436 people killed and 1,792 seriously wounded.

2 June
Hull's 50th air-raid.
22 June
Germany invades Russia.
10 July
Heinkel HE111H-5 crashes in sea off Hull, cause unknown.
11 July
Sharp attack on Hull causing widespread damage, major fires.
18 July
Heavy raid results in more than 150 fires with Reckitts, East Hull Gasworks and Spillers hit; 140 fatalities and 108 seriously injured.
6 August
King George VI and Queen Elizabeth visit Hull.
18 August
National Fire Service formed.
29-30 August
Junkers JU88 of 1(F)/120 crashes into sea after striking balloon cable over Humber.
30-31 August
Concentrated attack in which around 200 houses are destroyed.
22 September
'Tanks for Russia Week' begins in local factories.
1 December
German armour within nine miles of the Kremlin.
7 December
Japanese carrier planes attack US Pacific Fleet at Pearl Harbour, Hawaii. Japanese troops land in Malaya.
8 December
US and Britain declare war on Empire of Japan.
11 December
Germany and Italy declare war on the United States. War no longer confined to Europe and now a truly a global affair.

1942
2 February
Trawlers *Cape Spartel* and *Cloughton Wyke* bombed and sunk off Humber.
15 February
Singapore falls to Japanese.
19 May
Hull's heaviest raid of year leaves 50 killed and 58 seriously injured. Blackburn Aircraft factory at Brough suffers blast damage.
21 June
Tobruk falls to Rommell's Afrika Korps.
19 August
British and Canadian forces suffer heavy casualties during a Commando raid on Dieppe.
25 August
Duke of Kent killed in an air crash.
4 November
Afrika Korps defeated by British 8th Army at El Alamein.

1943
2 February
German 6th Army surrenders at Stalingrad.
9 March
German radio claims Hull extensively damaged by heavy raid. In fact, no bombs fell at all.
12 May
Axis forces in North Africa surrender.

13 June
3,000 anti-personnel bombs dropped on Grimsby and Cleethorpes, resulting in 74 people killed and 88 seriously injured.
10 July
Allies land in Sicily.
13 July
Hull raided, 26 killed but three of the attackers are destroyed.
24 July
RAF attack Hamburg with 740 aircraft.
25 July
German radio again claims heavy raid on Hull but again no bombs fell. Could this be for their home populations consumption due to Hamburg raid?
25 July
Essen raided by 627 aircraft.
27 July
Hamburg raided by 739 aircraft. Death toll amongst civilian population estimated at 20,000 men, women and children.
8 September
Italian surrender made public, although a secret armistice had been signed on the 3rd.
13 October
Italy declares war on Germany.
25 December
Trawler *Kingston Beryl* mined in north-western approaches.
22 January
Allies land at Anzio
20 April
German radio claims Hull blitzed. Again, no bombs fell.
6 June
Allies land in Normandy.
12-13 June
Start of VI rocket attacks against south-eastern England.
22 June
Russia launches summer offensive.
24 July
'Hitler salutes' made mandatory form of salute in German Army
1 August
Polish uprising in Warsaw. Poles massacred as Red Army does nothing to aid them.
25 August
Liberation of Paris.
30 August
Last VI launch sites overrun by British troops.
8 September
Start of V2 rocket attacks on London.
30 September
Part demobilization of National Fire Service. Those released are liable to military service or to be directed to industry.
3 December
Home Guard stood down.

1945
13 February
Undefended German city of Dresden attacked by 773 aircraft of the RAF. Estimated that 132,000 people killed.
7 March
US troops cross Rhine at Remagen.

17 March
Hull's last air-raid resulting in 12 killed and 22 seriously injured.
12 April
President Roosevelt dies.
23 April
Black-out restrictions lifted.
25 April
US and Soviet troops meet on the Elbe
28 April
Mussolini and his mistress executed by Italian partisans.
29 April
German forces in Italy surrender.
30 April
Hitler commits suicide. In his will he appoints Admiral Doenitz as Führer.
1 May
Britain's remaining ARP workers given one month's notice.
2 May
Hull trawler *Ebor Wyke* lost off Iceland. Sunk by U-boat?
4 May
Surrender of all German forces in North-West Europe.
8 May
VE Day in Britain.
13 May
Red Army offensive in Europe ends.
15 May
German troops in Yugoslavia surrender, estimated 30,000 Yugoslav collaborators then slaughtered by Tito's forces.
22 May
Rations cut in Britain.
23 May
Churchill resigns and forms 'caretaker' Government.
5 July
General Election in Britain.
10 July
Trawler *Kurd* mined off the Lizard.
26 July
Labour Party win General Election with 393 seats.
6 August
Atomic bomb dropped on Hiroshima
9 August
Atomic bomb dropped on Nagasaki.
14 August
Japanese surrender. German submarine U-977 arrives in Rio de la Plata, Argentina and surrenders. Rumours run wild that Adolf Hitler still alive, having been smuggled to Antarctica where he was already establishing a new Reich at New Berchtesgaden.
1 September
Clothing ration reduced by 25 per cent.
19 September
William Joyce ('Lord Haw Haw') sentenced to death for treason.
20 December
Labour controls end.